ACTIVATE HEAVEN

JOHN ECKHARDT

ACTIVATE HEAVEN

CHARISMA
HOUSE

Library of Congress Cataloging-in-Publication Data:
An application to register this book for cataloging has been submitted to the Library of Congress.
International Standard Book Number: 978-1-62999-862-6
E-book ISBN: 978-1-62999-863-3

21 22 23 24 25 — 9 8 7 6 5 4 3 2 1
Printed in the United States of America

CONTENTS

THE POWER OF YOUR SOUND

*How then shall they call on him in whom they
have not believed? and how shall they believe
in him of whom they have not heard? and
how shall they hear without a preacher? And
how shall they preach, except they be sent?*
—ROMANS 10:14–15

I LOVE PREACHERS. I love strong, powerful preachers. I have always wanted to do something special for preachers. At one time, I thought of hosting a preachers' conference to encourage them and, of course, get some of my favorite preachers in one room. There is a sound that really good preachers have. They know how to use their voices to stir the power and anointing of God. There's a range of pitches, resonance, vocal effects, volume, and revelations that are different for each one. Their unique sound stirs and inspires you, the listener, and releases you into your gifts and creativity.

But I have a word for you in this season that will really stretch and challenge you: God has given you a unique voice as well. There are things God has called you to speak and release into the earth that will break things open in people's lives that the enemy tried to say would be unbreakable. You have a sound that, just like your favorite preacher, heaven responds to. You may not consider yourself to be a preacher—and everyone does not need to be. You don't need to have a microphone and stand in a pulpit. You don't need a big megaphone. But as you begin to see past your limitations and use the power of your voice, God will take your voice where He wants it to go so it has the effect it was created to have. As a matter of fact, your voice can go places my voice or your favorite preacher's voice can't go. And you will "preach" in ways that only you can.

Romans 10:14 asks, "How shall they hear without a preacher?" The Greek word for *preacher* here is *kēryssō*, which means "preach," "publish," "proclaim," "to be a herald," "to publish, proclaim openly: something which has been done"—"the public proclamation of the gospel and matters pertaining to it."[1] In other words, preaching is not just about standing in a pulpit shouting a message to a congregation. Preaching is about using your voice in any public sphere to proclaim the gospel. We preach the gospel through writing and publishing books, prophesying, edifying and encouraging each other, decreeing and declaring the works of the kingdom in the earth, and praising and worshipping. The way we "preach" comes forth in ways that align our unique voice, gifts, and calling with the will and plan of God and that proclaim the goodness, mercy, and saving power of God. And it's not limited to what we do in church.

There's a lot to do outside of the church in the marketplace. So, again, I'm not just referring to whether you are a preacher or whether you are called to be a fivefold minister. This concept of "preaching" extends to businesspeople, marketplace people, and those in every realm of society. God may give you a mandate to operate in a sector of society outside the typical sphere of ministry. So I want to lay a foundation before we get into this full message, and that is this: God has given you certain gifts, talents, and abilities that all come together to form the unique sound you are designed to release in the earth. God has placed this very unique combination within you in order for you to contribute to the progress of this planet and humanity.

Many people live their lives without contributing to the progress and success of this planet and humankind. Many people live and die selfishly, thinking only of meeting their own needs and enjoying their own lives, never realizing they were born on purpose for a purpose. Not one of our lives was created by accident. Discovering and walking in our purpose is very important. So I want to first lay the foundation that you have a unique voice and place in the world that, when used, brings heaven down to earth. And when you contribute to the planet and humanity according to God's will by finding your purpose and walking in it, you will leave a blessing and legacy in the earth.

DO YOU HAVE EARS TO HEAR?

One of the difficult things in teaching this topic is that many believers are hesitant to use their unique position in the world because they are waiting for the planet to end. Their voices are silenced and shut up, and their gifts lie dormant because they have an end-of-the-world mentality. They think God is about to judge the planet and burn it up, so they really don't have a plan to contribute to it. Their plan is simply to go to heaven. Well, the Scriptures say in Matthew 5:5 and Psalm 37:11 that "the meek shall inherit the earth." And "the meek" are "those wholly relying on God rather than their own strength."[2] This should be all of us.

We who rely on the power of God inherit the whole earth and should be seeking God's plan for how we are to contribute to its success and that of all humanity. So, knowing this, we can also see how some of us must be delivered from religious teachings that have led to the belief that there is no use in contributing anything here since everything is about to end. We must get past the thinking that there's really nothing we can do about the earth and the things that happen in it and should just hold on until we go to heaven. We are to advance the kingdom of God, occupying more and more territory.

Jesus used the parable of the ten servants to teach us this principle of growing, investing, and stewarding our talents and gifts even while we await heaven. Luke 19:13 says, "And he called his ten servants, and delivered them ten pounds, and said unto them, Occupy till I come." When your time comes to stand before Him, will you hear, "Well done, thou good and faithful servant: thou hast been faithful over a few things, I will make thee ruler over many things: enter thou into the joy of thy lord" (Matt. 25:21)? Or will you argue with God about what you thought He wanted you to do with the time and talent you have in the here and now?

Don't get me wrong: I believe in heaven, and you should want to go there. I also believe the reason God saved you, redeemed you, and gave you talents, gifts, and abilities is for you to do something to further His plans and purposes, to be a deliverer, and to be a blessing.

We must remember that the message of salvation—the gospel—is not just to get us to heaven but also for us to live in victory, dominion, power, and abundance in this life. John 10:10 confirms this. Jesus says, "I am come that they might have life, and that they might have it more abundantly."

Another challenge for the people of God is knowing what they are called to speak into and how to activate and stir up the gifts through which they can speak. This is what you will be led to discover as you read this book.

There's still another area that often holds people back from using the power of their voice, and that is the area of shame and rejection. We will deal with this in a later chapter. If you have ever been told to shut up or sit down, that your voice doesn't matter, or that God doesn't hear you, you will be delivered from those words and released to speak as God gives you utterance.

SPECIAL AND CALLED OUT

There is so much God wants to release into the lives of His people concerning their authority, unique gifts, and voices. We have an effect on what happens in the earth. First Peter 4:10 says, "Just as each one of you has received a special gift [a spiritual talent, an ability graciously given by God], employ it in serving one another as [is appropriate for] good stewards of God's multi-faceted grace [faithfully using the diverse, varied gifts and abilities granted to Christians by God's unmerited favor]" (AMP). Bible teacher Guy Duininck explained it this way:

> The specific task God assigns each believer determines the specific variety of ministry grace He endows them

with. This truth is beautifully expressed by the Amplified Bible's rendering of Paul's words, "According to the grace (the special endowment for my task) of God bestowed upon me, like a skillful architect and master builder I laid [the] foundation..." (1 Cor. 3:10, AMP).

I don't know if the men who drafted the Amplified Bible were aware of the significant revelation about ministry grace they brought out in their rendering of 1 Corinthians 3:10. In any case, their amplification of the word "grace" is very accurate. They referred to grace as a "special endowment for [a] task."

God had assigned Paul a specific task. To enable him to fulfill that task, God specially endowed him. Paul's task was to lay spiritual foundations as a wise masterbuilder. The special endowment which enabled him to fulfill that task was the ministry grace God bestowed upon him.[3]

Israel was a special, chosen people (Deut. 14:2). Moses had a special assignment, and God gave him a special rod (Exod. 4:2). Samson was a special child, and God gave him special strength (Judg. 13:5; 16:16–17). Joseph had a special coat (Gen. 37:3) and a special assignment for which God gave him a special gift of interpreting dreams (Gen. 39–41). Bezaleel received a special gift to design parts of the tabernacle (Exod. 31:1–5). Elijah was a special prophet, and God gave him special faith to shut up the heavens (1 Kings 17). God gave Esther special favor because of her assignment (Est. 5). John the Baptist wore a special garment (Matt. 3:4), which some scholars believe was John's way of "reviving the outward appearance of Elijah," "whose copy he was." The garment signified the uniqueness of his call as a forerunning prophet.[4] The apostle Paul had a special assignment, and God performed special miracles through him (Acts 19:11). The apostle John had a special vision on the Isle of Patmos (Rev. 1).

"Compassed about with so great a cloud of witnesses" (Heb. 12:1), you have been chosen by God to do something significant, something that advances the kingdom, something special.

FINDING YOUR VOICE—HOW DO *YOU* PREACH?

We're going to talk about purpose, finding your calling, finding your destiny, and finding God's will for your life. Everyone's life preaches, but we don't all sound, look, or operate the same. You need to know your unique gifts and what God has imparted to you to preach heaven into lives full of hell. Through books like this you can receive ministry, impartation, activation, and release. You purchased this book, you are connecting with me, and now I have a part to play in helping you to discover the purpose and plan of God for your life. I have a responsibility to prophesy, impart, and activate the word of the Lord that may be lying dormant or just coming to fruition in your life.

Discovering God's plan concerning your unique way of releasing your voice is not as difficult as you may have thought. Many people stumble throughout life trying to figure out what God has called them to do and how He desires them to do it. "What is my purpose?" they'll ask over and over. "What is God's plan for my life? I'm having a hard time understanding it. Am I to do this? Am I to do that? What should I focus on? What should I give my time to?"

Maybe you struggle here too. I believe you can know God's will for you, and discovering it is not as difficult as you may think. This book is going to give you biblical counsel and a mighty release of the word of the Lord. Together we are going to believe God that something supernatural is going to be released in your life.

I pray today that God would give me wisdom, anointing, and the ability to articulate what is in my heart for you that you will have eyes to see, ears to hear, a heart to comprehend the messages that will be released in these pages concerning finding your voice, the call of God, and the purpose of God in your life.

GET READY FOR THE MUZZLE TO COME OFF

You are not just another man or woman stuck on the planet. You are seated in heavenly places in Christ. Have you heard the saying, "You're so heavenly minded that you're no earthly good"? I don't believe that. If you're heavenly minded, you do a lot of good on the earth. The problem is that we don't have enough heavenly minded people who know their identity and authority in Christ, who know the power of their voice to bring heaven to earth. We get so used to our prayer lines, prayer calls, and prayer circles within the four walls of the church that we forget the effectiveness of our words and the power of our voices in the earth. Real things happen when believers speak the word of the Lord.

It is time for heaven's voice to be heard on the earth. Let this be a new season when the muzzles come off and we begin to feel the word of the Lord burning within us like fire shut up in our bones.

Some things will not happen until you open your mouth. Your voice brings heaven to earth. When you open your mouth, heaven is speaking. When you prophesy, heaven is speaking. When you speak by the Spirit of God, heaven is speaking. No matter how much it seems like hell is raging, when you open your mouth, heaven comes.

When you open your mouth, the sick are healed and demons flee. Miracles and finances are released. When you speak, situations are turned around. Your voice will break every yoke and every barrier.

Speaking the will of God, speaking that which is in heaven, is the core of the prophetic realm. Therefore, stop complaining and begin to prophesy. Stop talking about how bad it is and begin to open your mouth and declare that as you speak, heaven comes.

When you show up, heaven shows up. You bring the glory of God. You bring power. You bring heaven. You bring the name that is above every name.

This book will impart to you the power of the voice of a believer, which advances the kingdom of God. You will learn how to speak with the virtue of Christ, which brings healing, deliverance, and salvation. When these miracle ministries are at work, the gospel is preached. How God has called you to participate in these miracle ministries demonstrates the numerous and unique ways you may preach the gospel. You will also learn the authority of your voice to halt and reverse the things of hell, those things that come to silence you. Depression, sadness, poverty, sickness, defeat, suicide, insanity, double mindedness, confusion, rejection, rebellion, pain, suffering—they have to go. If these demonic spirits have come in and stolen your confidence to speak with power and authority, you will learn how to get your voice back and walk in liberty.

You will gain a new understanding that reveals the prophetic connection between you and the heavens, which the

Bible says declare or speak forth the glory of God. Because of this revelation, a new boldness will arise in you and compel you to answer the Macedonian call. Then you will learn to steward the tongue to love wisdom and instruction.

It is time to break your silence and be released into a new boldness and confidence to preach the gospel in the way God has uniquely called you to. Your voice can go places you never imagined. Your words can be heard in nations you have never visited. Though the enemy has tried to limit your voice, your voice is not limited to your house, bedroom, or shower.

You may have been told to shut up, that you have nothing valuable to say, but God wants to use your voice. He has put a word of deliverance in your mouth. He has put a prayer of breakthrough on your lips and a prophetic message of salvation and healing on your tongue. Your voice has power.

It's time for your voice to be heard.

Chapter 1

THE HEAVENS DECLARE— YOU ARE THE HEAVENS

The heavens declare the glory of God; and the firmament shows His handiwork.

—Psalm 19:1, nkjv

I**T IS NOT** a common revelation that "the heavens" in this verse also refers to believers. Many understand that there are types and symbols in prophetic language, but few have uncovered the connection between the heavens declaring the glory of God and believers using their voices and words to proclaim the glory of God in the earth. This is really an amazing revelation in the Word of God about the power of our voices and the words we say.

I began to study this topic a while ago, and when I study, I also begin to write. Over time I had compiled a lot of research and thoughts on this revelation and began to preach it. So much freedom has come to people who have encountered this message—people who, again, have felt silenced, muzzled, shut down, and ignored. I believe a new freedom will also come to you as you receive this revelation. Understanding your position in heavenly places and what it means for you as you exist on the earth will have a profound effect on how you respond to your calling in God.

Throughout this chapter I'm going to share several verses to bring out this revelation. My primary text is going to be Psalm 19, but I am going to begin with a familiar verse out of Romans.

> Faith cometh by hearing, and hearing by the word of God.
> —ROMANS 10:17

You've likely heard this verse, probably hundreds of times. For me it became familiar because it was one of the major verses referenced in the Word of Faith movement, which I was exposed to in the early 1980s. It basically confirms that if you want faith, you must hear the Word of God through someone preaching it or by speaking it out of your mouth. That seems pretty simple. Then the next verse says:

> But I say, have they not heard? Yes indeed: "Their sound has gone out to all the earth, and their words to the ends of the world."
> —ROMANS 10:18, NKJV

Here, Paul was saying that in his generation, the gospel had been preached to the ends of the known world at that particular time, primarily referring to the Roman world, which included all of Europe, the Middle East, parts of Asia, and parts of North Africa—what we know as the Roman Empire. Most of that world at that time, Jews and Gentiles alike, had heard the gospel.

The apostles were being sent to all these different nations. Paul went to Rome. He had a desire to go to Spain and possibly France, which was called Gaul, but it is not known if he made it there. He and the apostles were sent out to all of Asia, Asia Minor, North Africa, and as far as Babylon. They preached the gospel in these regions and established churches.

So he was writing and asking, How could all these people hear the gospel without a preacher? And then how could preachers (the apostles at the time) preach except they be sent? Because "faith comes by hearing, and hearing by the word of God. But I say, have they not heard?" (Rom. 10:17–18, NKJV). And the answer was yes, they have heard, because "their sound has gone out to all the earth, and their words to the ends of the world" (Rom. 10:18, NKJV). The apostles had been preaching the gospel to the known world, and there was a real move of God in the first century.

But what's not often discussed and is very interesting about this passage in Romans 10 is that verse 18 is quoted from Psalm 19:4, all except one word. The Book of Romans says:

> Their voice has gone out to all the earth, and their words to the ends of the world.
> —ROMANS 10:18, ESV

As we saw previously, the New King James Version says:

> Their *sound* has gone out to all the earth, and their words to the ends of the world.
> —ROMANS 10:18, NKJV, EMPHASIS ADDED

The Book of Psalms says:

> Their voice goes out through all the earth, and their words to the end of the world.
>
> —PSALM 19:4, ESV

The King James Version says:

> Their *line* is gone out through all the earth, and their words to the end of the world.
>
> —PSALM 19:4, EMPHASIS ADDED

Voice. Sound. Line. The Hebrew word translated *line* (KJV) or *voice* (ESV) in Psalm 19:4 is connected to "a rim, a musical string or accord"; "the string of a harp; hence *sound*."[1] The Greek word translated "voice" or "sound" in Romans 10:18 is used to mean "musical sound, whether vocal or instrumental"; "utterance."[2]

When the everyday person reads Psalm 19, he or she may not see it as a representation of the gospel being preached. But evidently when Paul read it, the Spirit of God opened his eyes and understanding and told him that this was the fulfillment of a verse in Psalm 19.

Let's take a look at the first four verses of this psalm and notice what they tell us:

> The heavens declare the glory of God, and the sky above proclaims his handiwork. Day to day pours out speech, and night to night reveals knowledge. There is no speech ["nor language" is added in the KJV], nor are there words, whose voice is not heard. Their voice [or "line" in the KJV] goes out through all the earth, and their words to the end of the world. In them he has set a tent for the sun.
>
> —PSALM 19:1–4, ESV

I used to read this psalm and think it referred to the literal heavenly bodies God created—the sun, moon, and stars—and that the psalmist was saying their miraculous existence, their hanging there in the sky, testified of God's glory. I believe that's a good interpretation. When you look up into the heavens, the heavens declare God's glory. Yes.

I remember talking to a preacher who was raised in Bulgaria, which was once a Communist nation. He said that when he was growing up, he was not taught anything about God. It was against the law to preach the gospel in Bulgaria at that time. But when he looked in the sky, he said he knew there was a God. Even though laws can be passed attempting to stop the preaching of the gospel, you can't stop the stars from shining. You can't keep God out, because all you have to do is look to the heavens and see the sun, the moon, the stars—they declare the glory of God; they speak for God.

The Bulgarian preacher went on to say that even though it was against the law to hear or preach about God, he knew his government was telling him lies. Through the testimony of the stars, sun, and moon, God began to deal with him. He eventually received salvation and became a preacher.

In the same way as this preacher, I've always looked at Psalm 19 as saying the physical heavens—the sun, moon, and stars—are testaments to the glory of God. What's interesting, though, is that verses 2 and 3 say, "Day unto day uttereth speech, and night unto night sheweth knowledge. There is no speech nor language, where their voice is not heard." It seems as if this psalmist is prophesying about something bigger, something more than just the sun, moon, and stars, because he begins to talk about their voice.

The psalm continues: "Their line has gone out through

all the earth, and their words to the end of the world" (v. 4, NKJV). As I showed previously, this is the portion of the passage Paul quotes in Romans 10:18 regarding the preaching of the gospel. He saw apostolically and by revelation that Psalm 19 was a prophecy of the gospel being preached throughout the earth. It is about the actual preaching of the gospel, the sound of the voices of the preachers of the gospel, which causes faith to arise when it is heard. So this psalm is not just talking about the sun, moon, and stars. It is a proclamation about the day when the voice of the preacher would be heard in every nation.

In reading this, my questions were, Why would Paul open with writing about the heavens declaring the glory of God and then shift into the preacher's voice and their line going throughout the entire world? What is the connection between the heavens and the voice of the preacher? Why would Paul quote a prophetic word from Psalm 19 in Romans 10 and correlate it with the preaching of the gospel? How does Romans 10:18 connect with the heavens declaring the glory of God? Why would Paul quote that particular verse?

According to *Thayer's Greek Lexicon*, "Paul transfers what is said in Psalm 18:5 (Ps. 19:5) to the voices of the preachers of the gospel." [3] Who are the preachers of the gospel? According to Matthew 24:14 and Mark 16:15, we, as disciples of Christ, are "the preachers."

This is why we need revelation. There are some scriptures that from the surface say something we easily comprehend, yet our minds don't fully understand the deeper meanings. We need the Spirit of God to open up these mysteries to us, as some scriptures are saying something a bit different from what we would think.

So now, seeing that Paul put Psalm 19 in the context of the preaching of the gospel, you can understand that of course the sun, moon, and stars shine everywhere. There's no place where they don't shine. However, could it be that at times the Lord uses "heavens" not just to refer to the physical heavens but also to refer to His people? Could it be that in connecting this to the voice of the believer, which is sent out from God and commissioned by Him, there is no place where *our* voices will not be heard?

It has been eye opening to me and so many others to explore the possibility that it is not just the heavens that declare, but it is also you who declare, speak, proclaim, herald, publish, and announce the saving gospel of the kingdom. I see it as another expression of our identity as believers. This is where I began to declare, "I am the heavens." You are the heavens the psalmist was writing about. Through Paul's transference, as *Thayer's* points to, you and I—our voices—are the heavens that shine and declare the glory of God and go throughout the earth. Several more passages in Psalms continue this theme.

Psalm 89:5 says, "And the heavens will praise Your wonders, O LORD" (NKJV). The heavens praise. Psalm 96:11 says, "Let the heavens rejoice" (NKJV). Then Psalm 148:1 says, "Praise the LORD! Praise the LORD from the heavens; praise Him in the heights" (NKJV). And verse 4 of that chapter says, "Praise Him, you heavens of heavens, and you waters above the heavens" (NKJV). Then Psalm 103:19 says, "The LORD hath prepared his throne in the heavens; and his kingdom ruleth over all." This last verse is interesting, because according to Luke 17:21, the kingdom of God is in us. The kingdom has a throne, and Psalm 103:19 says the throne is in the heavens, which according to Paul's new covenant revelation is us.

The parallels between a believer's voice and identity in Christ and the heavens declaring speaks to the unique nature of prophetic language. If you recall, prophetic language gives us insight into biblical types and shadows of the old covenant and how they foretold of the new covenant realities fulfilled through Christ. The Law, Passover, Pentecost, Day of Atonement, dietary laws, circumcision, sabbaths, and the like were all shadows. Christ brought to us the reality and fullness of these Old Testament laws, customs, and ordinances.

I believe that the heavens declaring serves as an "example and shadow of heavenly things" (Heb. 8:5) and point to "a shadow of good things to come" (Heb. 10:1) for God's people. So when Psalm 19 makes mention of the sun, moon, and stars, I believe that it is not speaking of "the very image of the things" (Heb. 10:1), but that they are types and shadows of who we are in Christ.

We see this further in Daniel 4:26, which says, "And whereas they commanded to leave the stump of the tree roots; thy kingdom shall be sure unto thee, after that thou shalt have known that the heavens do rule." The heavens rule. The heavens praise. The heavens rejoice. We also praise, rule, and rejoice.

So these references to the heavens declaring the glory of God, the heavens praising, ruling, rejoicing, and speaking are not only about the physical realities of the heavens but also are pointing to the spiritual realities that exist for His people. Through this prophetic language we are being given greater depth into who we are and where our realm of authority lies. Our sound and voice are heard throughout the world. The Scriptures say that we sit in heavenly places in Christ Jesus

(Eph. 2:6). That is our position. The kingdom of God is from heaven and is in us.

As I pondered verses that say, "Praise the Lord, heavens," I would look up to heaven and question, "Are they praising God? Are the sun, moon, and stars clapping and praising God?" Then I thought about how the Bible says that the trees clap their hands (Isa. 55:12), how it calls us "trees of righteousness" (Isa. 61:3), or when it says, "Let the sea roar" (Ps. 98:7). *Sea* represents nations.[4] We can then read the verse as saying, "Let the *nations* roar."

So, again, seeing the connection between Psalm 19:4 and Romans 10:18—the heavens declaring and the voice of the preacher/believer—is about understanding prophetic terminology we sometimes miss. Sometimes we try to understand Scripture, yet we don't understand prophetic language, and we read everything literally.

WHEN YOU SPEAK, HEAVEN SPEAKS

Sometimes we don't realize who we are until the Spirit of God shows us in Scripture. The revelation Paul had concerning Psalm 19 is to let you know you're not just anybody. Let me say it this way: When you speak by the Spirit of God, heaven is speaking. Heaven is declaring. Heaven is uttering its voice. Heaven is decreeing. Then as we saw in Psalm 103:19, heaven rules over all, which means that we, as the people of God, walk in authority.

In the natural, the heavens rule over the earth. But spiritually, we are the heavens that rule over the earth. It's time for the people of God to realize we're not just another person stuck on the planet. We are sitting in heavenly places in Christ. We are the heavens God spoke of, and it is time for heaven's voice to be heard on the earth. There's been enough of listening to earth's voice. It is time for heaven's voice to be heard, and we are—you are—heaven's voice.

SPEAK AS GOD SPEAKS THROUGH YOU

When you open your mouth by the Spirit of God, it is not you speaking; it is God. Wherever you go, you need to bring heaven. No matter how much hell the enemy has tried to bring in, when you open your mouth, heaven comes. When you open your mouth by the Spirit of God, the sick get healed, demons come out, miracles happen, and finances are released. When heaven gets involved, no matter how messed up a situation is, things begin to turn around.

The anointing of heaven breaks every yoke. It breaks every barrier. People need that word from heaven. When you open your mouth and stop complaining and begin to prophesy, heaven shows up. Stop talking about how bad it is and begin to open your mouth like the heavens and declare the word of the Lord.

Know that when you step into someone's life, heaven shows up. As I said in the introduction, you bring the glory and power of God. You bring heaven's authority. When you as a child of God show up on the scene, heaven shows up. We read where the Bible says that the heavens rule over everything. What that says to me is that no matter how many demons are there, when you show up, they have to go.

Have you ever heard somebody say, "My life is a living hell"? Do not agree with that kind of thinking. Declare that you are the heavens and that when you show up, heaven shows up. Sometimes in our desire to empathize and show compassion, we downplay the power that is living inside us. Refuse to let demons of hell run your life. Declare glory, prosperity, anointing, healing, power, joy, salvation, praise, worship, dancing, celebrating, the anointing, the presence of God, and the Word of God over your life. These are the things of heaven. These are the things that should follow you everywhere you go.

KNOW WHO YOU ARE

It is so important that you get this, because the devil will make you think you are just another person down here trying to make it. You aren't. The kingdom of God, which is heaven, resides in you. The problems we experience so often boil down to the fact that we don't know our identity in Christ. We don't really know who we are. We don't know what really happens when we open our mouths. We don't know what really happens when we begin to sing about the anointing of God. We don't understand what's really happening when we prophesy. We can get so used to these spiritual activities that we just take them for granted, and we forget the power we have in our voices.

The devil uses this and tries to put a muzzle on our mouths. He tries to make us think we can't say anything, or if we do, it won't make a difference. But I pray that if you come close to shutting up, you'll feel like Jeremiah, like there is fire shut up in your bones.

> If I say, "I will not mention his word or speak anymore in his name," his word is in my heart like a fire, a fire shut up in my bones. I am weary of holding it in; indeed, I cannot.
>
> —JEREMIAH 20:9, NIV

Every person or circumstance that the enemy used to tell you to sit down and not say anything must not have known that you can't shut up heaven. Those devices of the enemy that tried to limit your voice by communicating that your voice is not important, that you can't go far, that you are just limited to preaching a small sermon to a small group of people do not know the power of heaven in your voice.

What's happening now—and there are some not-so-good things about it—is that everybody has a phone and their own "TV" program called Facebook Live, Instagram Live, YouTube, Periscope, and others. There is no reason for any of us to remain silent when God has put a word in our mouths.

OPEN YOUR MOUTH

God has given you a voice that reverberates in the heavens, and I am writing this book to help you activate your voice. So much within our lives is voice activated. Some things won't happen until you open your mouth. Like Job 22:28 says, you shall decree a thing, and it will be established. You can speak to mountains and they will be removed and cast into the sea. The mountains will obey you. There are some things that don't happen until heaven speaks. Don't sit there and be quiet. You'd better learn how to talk back to the devil. You'd better learn how to rebuke the devil and take authority over the mountains he puts in your way. You'd better learn how to open your mouth and prophesy, because some things will not happen until your voice is released.

God is going to take the muzzle off your mouth. He's going to break that spirit of fear that keeps you from saying what He wants you to say. He is going to break that assignment of hell against your voice and the major demons set against our voices.

Right now, the devil may have you afraid to say what God says, but you cannot be afraid. You must speak boldly and with courage. You must speak with faith (in another chapter I will teach more on virtues such as faith and how they cause us to stay on track with God).

At one time, I used to preach something that was against what is traditionally preached, and I was afraid to preach it. One day I said, "God, if I say this, I'm going to get in trouble."

God said, "Say it."

When I preached that message, it brought deliverance and healing to the people who heard it. It was not an easy message. It was a word that could have led people to send me all kinds of complaints and disapproval.

Those who followed Jesus heard Him say things like, "For My flesh is food indeed, and My blood is drink indeed. He who eats My flesh and drinks My blood abides in Me, and I in him" (John 6:55–56, NKJV). We see Jesus' words as symbolic, but His disciples took them literally: "This is a hard saying; who can understand it?" (v. 60, NKJV). What man of God would ask people to take part in cannibalism? Jesus said things people couldn't handle.

But God gave you a voice, and when you open your mouth and use it, people get delivered, healed, and restored. Your voice will bother demons, because you are the heavens. When heaven speaks, demons hate it. It takes a voice speaking with the authority of heaven to cast out devils, to tell them, "Come out."

Jesus spoke to winds and waves because He knew who He was. You must become comfortable with the sound of your voice, the unique way that you are meant to declare the glory of God. This is what we will discover throughout this book. But before we go on, let's make some decrees.

DELIVERANCE FROM ATTACKS AGAINST YOUR VOICE

I want you to put your hand on your voice box and read these decrees aloud:

In the name of Jesus, there's a new anointing coming on my voice and onto my words.

I receive a fresh anointing to speak as the oracle of God.

From this day forward, when I open my mouth, I believe miracles will be released. Every time I open my mouth, I expect a miracle.

Your finances are about to change. Your mind is about to change. Your family is about to change. Your ministry is about to change. You will prophesy to your city or your nation, and the government and economy will change, because you opened your mouth and decreed it.

The Lord is saying that your voice is about to change things. Now, pray:

Lord, thank You for releasing my voice. Every demon that has come against my voice, I rebuke you, in the name of Jesus. You cannot kill my voice. You cannot stop my voice. You cannot hinder my voice. Every spirit that has attacked my voice, I rebuke you. My voice is loose, in the name of Jesus. Amen.

CHAPTER 2

THE MACEDONIAN MANDATE

*A vision appeared to Paul in the night. A man
of Macedonia stood and pleaded with him,
saying, "Come over to Macedonia and help us."*
—ACTS 16:9, NKJV

A

S YOUR VOICE is calibrated to bring the blessing, deliverance, and shalom of heaven, your sound is needed in every corner of the earth. In our age, building a platform seems to be on every person's mind. Getting on Facebook Live and preaching, singing, and training whomever may stop scrolling and listen is what so many are doing to reach as many people as possible. They desire to get their message out to as many as they can. Often this can be a point of competition: Who has the most followers? Who has the most viewers? Who is drawing the most attention and getting other opportunities to speak, preach, teach, or share their skills and expertise?

Now, I'm not saying any of this is wrong, but I want you to know that God knows how to get your voice out. God knows how to release your voice. He knows where your word needs to go. As He purifies and matures your voice, He will bring promotion and set you before great men and women. He may give you a prophetic word for somebody. He may cause you to have a dream, like the apostle Paul did, of somebody saying, "Come over to our church, come over to our company, come over to our nation and help us. We need to hear your voice."

In Acts 16, Paul had a dream of a man pleading with him to come to Macedonia and help them. Paul had never been to Macedonia, but the man had asked him to come over to Macedonia and help them. So Paul went to Macedonia, preached the word of God, and revival broke out. His voice needed to be heard in Macedonia. There may be places you've never been, but God can come to you in a dream and tell you where to go. He can show you people in your dream whom He wants you to contact to give them a word.

The apostle Peter provides another example of God speaking in a dream about where someone should go to deliver His word. In Acts 10:9–23, Peter had a vision of a sheet coming down from heaven, of unclean animals that represented unclean nations—Gentiles. Immediately following the vision, God sent a messenger from the house of the Roman centurion Cornelius to Peter. The messenger asked Peter to go with him to Cornelius' house. Arriving there, Peter preached, and the Spirit of God fell on all who were in the house (Acts 10:44). They began to speak in tongues, and all of a sudden, the floodgates were open. As a result of their conversion, more Gentiles began to come into the church along with the Jewish believers.

As we've seen from Paul's and Peter's examples, your voice can go places you've never been. God can do it through dreams. God can do it through visions. God can speak to you. He can even have somebody call you.

I got a call once. It wasn't on my phone; it was through Facebook Messenger. I wasn't used to receiving calls that way, but I answered.

"Hello? Who is this?" I asked.

A guy with an accent answered and said, "Praise the Lord! Apostle Eckhardt, I am calling from Moldova."

Moldova? Moldova is in Eastern Europe, near Russia.

He said, "Praise the Lord! I got your book. I've been reading your book. I'm an evangelist in Moldova. I want you to pray for me."

I said, "OK."

I've never been to Moldova. I don't know anybody there. But somehow my book was there.

The man then said, "I'm a Russian evangelist. I speak English. When I preach in Russian, we go on the streets. I've been reading your books on the apostolic. Would you bless me?"

I said, "Well, if you had the nerve to call me from Moldova on Facebook, I'm going to pray for you."

I began to pray for him, and I prophesied over him on the phone through Facebook Messenger. He received the prophetic word, and my voice was going into Moldova—from the South Side of Chicago to Moldova.

Have you ever been to Moldova? Not many people have. I learned it is near Transylvania. I was in Hungary once, and my hosts pointed in a direction and said, "There's Transylvania."

I said, "Transylvania? Isn't that where Dracula is from?"

They said, "Yes. There are many witches there."

I said, "Well, God bless Transylvania. I am not going up

there, dealing with Herman and Eddie Munster and Dracula. No, thank you. I am OK. I've dealt with witchcraft, but I don't want to deal with Transylvanian witchcraft."

The point here is that you can end up in strange places—places you've never been—as God begins to send you to people who need what you have.

RISE, SHINE, AND COME FORTH

Some time ago I was leading a congregation through a series of prophetic activations. We were doing one activation where we encourage people to hear the sound of the Lord. When you are tuned in to the Spirit in this way, sometimes the Lord gives you sounds. You may hear wind blowing, rain falling, or birds singing. You may hear trains. This time, I heard the sound of an army marching. In the spirit, I heard its boots marching. Then the Lord gave me a verse in Psalm 68. It says, "The Lord gave the word: great was the company of those that published it" (v. 11).

The Hebrew word translated "company" means "army."[1] It is also translated as an army of women in some Bible versions.[2] Somehow the King James Version left that out. Some people don't think women can preach or prophesy, but every married man knows women preach.

So as I was leading this activation, I began to see how America needs revival and breakthrough. There is so much going on in our country—perversion, rebellion, witchcraft, violence, hatred, and injustice. It's amazing. But I believe that when it's the darkest, that's when prophetic people rise.

Elijah was the prophet when Jezebel was ruling the nation. Two of the most wicked people who have ever ascended to the throne, Ahab and Jezebel, were the ones controlling the nations, but God raised up Elijah. God has a way of raising up strong anointings when the world seems dark, when it looks like the devil is taking over and witchcraft is prevailing. The strongest anointings are raised up when things are bad. Strong people are raised up who know how to pray and fast, preach and teach—people who know how to rebuke, take authority, and prophesy.

I believe no matter how dark it looks, the Bible says, "Arise, shine; for thy light is come, and the glory of the Lord is risen upon thee. For, behold, the darkness shall cover the earth, and gross darkness the people: but the Lord shall arise upon thee, and his glory shall be seen upon thee" (Isa. 60:1–2).

When darkness tries to cover the land, that is when it is time for you to shine, rise, and come forth. God is raising up a new breed of believers who will prophesy, pray, preach, teach, bind, and loose. He is raising up a company of people who know that no weapon formed against us shall prosper. When the enemy comes in like a flood, the Spirit of the Lord will raise a standard against him (Isa. 59:19).

No matter how bad it looks, one word can turn a situation around. All it takes is one word from God to change a whole situation. So this concept of being a voice, being the heavens, or having a voice that activates heaven is not just people saying, "Thus saith the Lord." It's about an army of believers God is raising up, an army into whose mouths God will put His word so that when they release it, something will shake and change.

Things are changing politically. There is a lot of division, particularly in America. Everybody hates everybody, it seems. We have problems with people in the military, with the police department, with authority, with racism, with prejudice, with

Democrats versus Republicans, and with drugs. Since the COVID-19 pandemic, so many things have come undone and need to be set back in order. But I believe God is going to send those with His words—with solutions, skill, wisdom, and insight—and we will see that the best is yet to come.

HOW YOU "SPEAK" IS UNIQUE

Some of us are more evangelistic—we feel a sense of urgency to use our voices, gifts, and talents to introduce people to the gospel of Jesus. Some of us are more apostolic—we feel motivated to use our voices, gifts, and talents to help establish systems and programs that secure the church or other organization they've been put in place to serve. Some of us use our voices, gifts, and talents to teach, coach, mentor, or train. Others of us use our voices, gifts, and talents to serve, administrate, give, or pastor.

Each of us "speaks" with our different gifts and graces. We're not the same. Even two apostles can be different. Even two prophets can be different. Don't try to be like someone else. Be what God has called you to be. Go where He sends you. Don't be a copycat. Don't be a clone. It's OK to receive an impartation from someone, but God has created you to be different and unique. Don't be born an original and die a copy. We have too many copies out here.

As God prepares you to go to your Macedonia, know that you may seem different than what people expect, or the place He's called you to go may be different from where some people think you ought to go. Expect to be misunderstood.

SPECIAL ASSIGNMENTS, CALLINGS, AND MANDATES

When you walk in a special grace, special anointing, special ability, or special talent, it opens you up to the realm of what I call special miracles. There is a class of miracles called special miracles. You can find evidence of this in Acts 19:11, which says, "And God wrought special miracles by the hands of Paul." This is telling us that there is the miracle realm, and then there is the special miracle realm. The word *special* simply means something unusual, something better, or something on a higher level. In the New King James Version the same verse says, "Now God worked *unusual* miracles by the hands of Paul" (emphasis added).

As you walk in this new heavenly identity, you need to understand how important it is that the Lord performs special miracles for you and through you. This is how you demonstrate the things that are in heaven that can be loosed in others' lives. This is also how God will bless you so that by your words and actions—your hands—the special miracles of heaven will be released into the lives of those God sends you to.

For you and through you, God wants to do something different, something unusual. He wants to perform some unusual miracles. He wants to open some unusual doors. He wants to bring unusual breakthroughs. He wants to raise you to unusual levels. He wants to cause you to make unusual connections. He wants to do something very unusual for you and through you.

In studying the word *special*, you will find that it is not a word frequently used in the King James Version. It is more often used in other translations such as the Amplified Bible, the Voice translation, the Passion Translation, and the Living Bible. Then if you follow how the word is used, you will see it show up as "special messenger"—the apostles were called special messengers. You will see references to "special favor," which was given to Esther. But when we see "special endowments," the word is being used to describe an unusual impartation of the gifts of the Spirit. The apostle Peter talks about this.

> As each of you has received a gift (a particular spiritual talent, a gracious divine endowment), employ it for one another as [befits] good trustees of God's many-sided grace [faithful stewards of the extremely diverse powers and gifts granted to Christians by unmerited favor].
> —1 PETER 4:10, AMPC

Paul told Timothy to stir up the gift, or the special endowment, that was given to him by prophecy with the laying on of hands of the presbytery.

> Do not neglect the gift which is in you, [that special inward endowment] which was directly imparted to you [by the Holy Spirit] by prophetic utterance when the elders laid their hands upon you [at your ordination].
> — 1 TIMOTHY 4:14, AMPC

Spirit-filled ministry, especially prophecy and the laying on of hands, is a vehicle through which gifts or special endowments are released into your life. Then in 2 Timothy 1:6, Paul told Timothy again to neglect not the gift God had given through the laying on of his hands.

Special endowments come directly from God through the vehicle of laying on of hands in prophecy. These are unique gifts: prophecy, tongues, interpretation of tongues, faith, gifts of healing, the working of miracles, word of knowledge, word of wisdom, discerning of spirits, mercy, giving, exhortation, prophecy, serving, and so on. (See Romans 12.) All of these special endowments are connected to the miraculous—when you move in words of knowledge, words of wisdom, and discerning of spirits; and when you prophesy, speak in tongues, or interpret tongues. Moving in these gifts releases miracles, as they are imparted as special abilities to individuals with special assignments, commissions, or mandates.

As I mentioned at the beginning of this chapter, Paul had a special commission to preach to the Gentiles. One of the places he went, Macedonia, became known to him through a dream. To help Paul carry out the mission God assigned to him, God gave him an endowment of special miracles. You're reading this because God has given you a special assignment—a place where your voice will have great impact. It doesn't mean God is calling you to a worldwide platform, but your assignment is something special. It can be in the local church or the marketplace, politics or media. Whether it is national or international, it is a special assignment. God has given you a unique way to speak and preach heaven. He has given you special vision and a special gift. This thing that God has placed within you is unique and different, and it separates you from others.

REMAIN HUMBLE

My calling out your uniqueness is not an attempt to feed your pride or a statement that you are better than anyone else. The truth is, the more special you and the things God does in your life are, the more humility you must have. God gave Paul a special mandate to preach to the Gentiles but then gave him a thorn in the flesh, because the abundance of revelations given to him could have caused him to be puffed up. (See 2 Corinthians 12:7–10.) He had to walk in humility and depend on the grace of God. Paul received special revelation from heaven. He understood the mysteries of God more than all the other apostles. There was special grace given to him, but there was also a thorn in his flesh to keep him in a place of humility.

God does give special gifts, special talents, and special anointings—and we need them if we want to bring heaven into the lives of so many who are living in a kind of hell on earth—but these endowments are never given to make us think we are better than someone else. What we can recognize is that God does give people special assignments, special callings, and special mandates—special things to do on behalf of the kingdom—and they may be different, unusual, and not standard. Often when God gives us those kinds of mandates, we tend to pull back because we've never seen something quite like it before.

Think of this: John the Baptist was a special messenger raised up by God. (See John 1:5–15.) After he was born, people wanted to name him after his father, Zacharias, but God said, "His name is John."

Zacharias may have thought, "But there's no one in my family named John."

Zacharias and those around him didn't understand that God wanted the child to be named John because he was special. He was different. He was unique. He had a special calling. He carried the spirit of Elijah. He was in the wilderness eating locusts and wild honey. He had a special garment of goats' hair. God was raising up a special kind of ministry to be the forerunner of Christ.

Samson was different. He was special. When Samson was a child, God said, "Don't cut his hair. He's going to be a Nazarite. He can't drink any wine, because he's special." (See Judges 13:5, 7.) God gave him special strength to use to bring deliverance to Israel.

Then there was Joseph. His father made him a special coat of many colors because he was different from his brothers. (See Genesis 37:3.) He had a special assignment to go into Egypt before them and bring deliverance to his family. He had a special endowment—the ability to interpret dreams. It was something very unusual; no matter how difficult the dream was, he had a special endowment to interpret it.

God also gave Daniel and the Hebrew boys a special endowment of wisdom, knowledge, and interpretation of dreams.

Then God gave Solomon a special endowment of wisdom. Solomon received a special ability to walk in wisdom more than any other person of his day, and really, anyone in history. No one could come close to matching the endowment God gave to Solomon.

And there was the special endowments God gave Bezaleel: the special skill and wisdom to construct the articles of the tabernacle and to design the garments of the priests and the tabernacle. (See Exodus 31:1–6.)

John the Baptist was different. Samson was different. Joseph was different. Daniel and the three Hebrew boys were different. Solomon and Bezaleel were different, and so are you.

HOW HAVE YOU BEEN GIFTED?

Through the Holy Spirit you can receive a special endowment, something that is unusual, unique, and on a different level. Oftentimes this endowment comes when you get baptized in the Holy Spirit. This is why we need to understand that being filled with the Spirit of God is more than just speaking in tongues and more even than just prophesying. We've been limited sometimes in Pentecostal and Charismatic churches when we limit the Spirit of God to just speaking in tongues. And then when these unusual gifts are operating in people, many leaders don't know how to govern, help, raise up, release, or send out those individuals, because religion always tries to make everyone the same. Some leaders don't know how to handle individuals the way Paul handled Timothy when he told him not to neglect that special endowment but to stir it up.

What special endowment has God given you? What word has He put in your mouth? To what people are you sent? What of heaven are you commissioned to bring to them? What has God given you? Maybe you're a writer, singer, or songwriter. Maybe you're an administrator or a creative. Maybe you're innovative, a businessperson, someone with cutting-edge ideas that generate wealth and income. Maybe God gave you the ability to devise inventions or to learn and grab on to knowledge quickly. Maybe you can speak different languages and learning languages comes quickly to you.

You may have a special ability to work in prisons or with the homeless, the poor, or single mothers. You may have a special calling to work with those who've been raped or molested. These are unique, special endowments that come from heaven. They require patience and long-suffering—two of the virtues that should accompany anyone who is being sent out for special assignments. I'll discuss those virtues further in chapters 6 and 7.

When we operate in our unique assignments with the

endowment that God has given us, we will begin to see the miracles of God. Many people are going to be blessed and delivered. They will see you operating in the gifting and anointing of God, and they're going to understand these are endowments from God and are going to see the glory of God. Your gifts declare—preach, proclaim, and make public—the glory of God. You are the heavens.

Remember, God gave wisdom, knowledge, and understanding to the Hebrew boys in Babylon, making them ten times better in their learning ability and comprehension of science and math than all those in Babylon. When they operated in their gifts, they brought blessing and prosperity to that nation, and the king of the land knew it was the God of Israel who empowered them.

WHO WILL THEY CALL?

Sometimes we try to put a certain name on something that God has a different name for. Sometimes you're even different from your family. I was the first person in my family to get saved. No one in my family—not my mother, father, or anyone else I knew—was saved. They were good people, but I did not have the example of other believers in my family. I never heard of anyone speaking in tongues or prophesying. I never saw anyone lift their hands. I'd never met a saved person until I was twenty years of age. I had no saved friends, and no one had ever witnessed to me. I didn't go to church, and so I got saved at a street meeting. A team came out and preached, and I got convicted and saved.

I was then the first person in my family to be born again, the first person to ever speak in tongues and become Spirit-filled, so I didn't have any point of reference. There was no one I could talk to in my family, so all my friends laughed at me. My family thought I was crazy because I started going to a Pentecostal church.

The saved life was new to me. I didn't know one verse in the Bible, not even John 3:16. But then God began to save my family members. God began to save my friends. The same ones who laughed at me asked me to pray for them. The same people who laugh at you will be the ones who come to you when they need a breakthrough. They know who to call. They may call you fanatical. They may tell you, "It doesn't take all that." But when they get in trouble, they'll be dialing your phone number. They'll be hitting you up to say, "You need to pray for me."

I once met a pastor who didn't believe in speaking in tongues. He was a good man and a good pastor, but he didn't believe in those things. Then one day he got in trouble, so he called me and said, "I need you to pray for me. I'm in trouble."

Because I knew he didn't believe in speaking in tongues, I started praying in English. "Heavenly Father, I just pray..."

He said, "No, no. I can do that. I can pray in English for myself. I need you to pray in tongues."

Your call to be the voice that activates heaven may lead you to live in a way people think is strange. It may cause you to do things for the Lord that people won't understand. But let them get in trouble; they know whom to call. They know who has the power. They know who can get a prayer through. They know who can cast out a devil. They know who walks in authority. They can laugh at you until they get in trouble. They're not going to ask some religious person to pray for them. They are going to pass by everyone else to find you, because you're different, and God made you that way.

REJECT SELF-REJECTION

Sometimes when you're different, you're not understood. You're not received. One of the worst demons that you can have is not just rejection; it's self-rejection. Sometimes people who've been rejected get a demon of self-rejection, where they reject themselves based on what others think about them. Stand strong in your identity as one who has influence in the heavens, and don't base your opinion on what other people think about you. Hold tight to the revelation of who God made you to be. You're not like everybody.

Like Joseph, who was different from his brethren, there's a different anointing on your life. As I mentioned, Joseph had a coat of many colors that his father, Jacob, made him. He was the favorite son. This led his brothers to hate him. So they took him and sold him as a slave into Egypt. Then when he got there, he was lied about and thrown in prison, where he was forgotten until one day when Pharaoh had a dream.

Something about Joseph was different. He was a righteous man. He was a godly man. He was raised around a bunch of brothers who saw something in him that they didn't like, but one day the same people who sold him had to come to him for help. (See Genesis 42.)

God will make your enemies your footstool. They may hate you and talk about you, but when there's a call of God on your life, you may be the one God uses to deliver the same people who didn't understand you. Don't reject yourself. Accept who God has called you to be. Thank God for making you different, unique, and special.

YOUR DIFFERENCE BRINGS CHANGE

What I want to tell you here is something I learned at a young age: you may be different, but that is exactly how God makes people—different. God put a unique anointing on your life, so stop trying to be like everybody else.

I'm not talking about being weird. No; I'm talking about the fact that you think differently, that you're wired differently. God put a unique anointing on your life. I've discovered that if things are to change in our lives, our families, our communities, or the world, we must realize that change doesn't usually come until someone different comes, because when everybody's the same, things remain the same. So don't let religious leaders shut you down or try to control your unique gifts. Find a church where there is liberty and freedom, where they will show you how you can use your gift to advance the kingdom. Then watch how God will use that special endowment to release things in your life and in the lives of others and cause you to do things that are unusual, different, and on another level.

Samson was a different kind of child. Joseph was different. Samuel was different. David was different. Jeremiah was different. Moses was different. These people just had different graces and different anointings on their lives. God wants to use your difference and uniqueness to really bring change to your generation. So I want to encourage you to learn how to flow in the power of God. Embrace the difference in your sound, your voice, and the area to which God has called you. Walk into your Macedonia, where you are needed. It may not be within the four walls of the church like some others are called to. Both Paul and Peter were called to different places to minister to people many thought weren't qualified to hear the gospel. Their ministry in those unique places to a unique people was different and new. God called them to those places as foreigners, as difference makers and change agents, and revival broke out.

Now as you are called out, accept who you are, move in the prophetic, and let God use you to bring change, deliverance, and healing. And don't be surprised in the days to come when you see endowments and gifts you've not seen before.

PROPHESYING YOUR MACEDONIA MOMENT

The Lord is saying:

> Even though you may have seen much, I'm going to do unusual things. You will be shocked at all the things you'll see. In the days to come, I will release not just endowments but special and unique endowments and abilities beyond what you've seen before. And you will say, "I've never seen that kind of anointing. I've never seen that kind of gift."
>
> It will be unusual, and to some, it will appear strange. It will be unorthodox, but it will release miracles and breakthroughs, finances and wealth, success, and new levels to the ones I am sending. For I am the God who gives wisdom. I am the God who gives knowledge and understanding. I am the God who gives special abilities.
>
> It will be as it was in the days of Solomon and as it was in the days of their captivity when I gave My special ones, My chosen ones, endowments, so much so that their wisdom and knowledge were recognized in the kingdoms in which they lived and were held captive. The gifts and talents that are placed in you, even today as you go out to serve, will cause corporations and businesses to

recognize the gifts that are placed in you, even administrative gifting and management. Endowments shall come, and they will call upon you as they called upon Joseph, Daniel, and Solomon. As they drew from the endowments placed inside of them, they will draw from the endowments in you, and those who need answers and solutions, even to difficult problems, they will be solved by the wisdom, knowledge, understanding, and revelation I give you in this era.

Don't limit Me, and don't limit Me to what you've seen in the past. Know that you will see unusual things. You will see special manifestations of My power, My glory, My gifts, My abilities, and you will do things you've not seen done before. You will do things that have never been done in your family. You will see things in your church and ministry that you've never seen before.

Even though you've seen much, get ready, for special anointing, special miracles, and even special assignments and mandates will come. They will be revealed through the prophetic flow and through prophecy and the laying on of hands. For I'm going to visit and dwell in places that are open to My Spirit and My function. I'm going to dwell among people who believe Me for the unusual and people who are open to My Spirit. I'm going to dwell and manifest strong on the behalf of those who are ready to receive the new thing I desire to do.

Get ready for a release of My word. Unusual dreams and insight will come even from My Word, and you will see new and unusual things happen in the way that you preach, teach, and prophesy. Many people have limited the apostolic and prophetic, saying it must operate this way or it must operate that way. But even as I raised up special prophets like Elijah, Moses, and John, and special apostles like Paul, in this hour, I break the limitations of what you believe it is to be an apostle or a prophet. Yes, you will walk in the signs of an apostle that are in My Word, but I will even raise up unique anointings and unique abilities and send you to unique places. I will cause you to do special things, I will release special miracles into your hands, and you will see special breakthroughs.

As I gave unusual and special endowments to the Hebrew boys and Daniel, I do it for you in this hour. I changed not. As I did it then, I can do it now. Don't look at what I did for them as just a history of what I did then. I am the same today, yesterday, and forever. As I put My Spirit in them and gave them My Spirit, I give it to you. So, receive it and walk in that special gift, talent, and ability. Walk in humility and know that it is from Me.

What I give you is not something that can be given by man. It comes in by My Spirit and then flows out of the humble ones—those who love Me, those who trust Me, those who receive from Me. Do not be puffed up, but walk in grace and humility, and you will see yourself doing things others have not done before.

Many will ask you, "How did you do that?" And you will give Me the praise and say, "It's God's gift. It's God's talent. It's God's ability. For I am the God who gives gifts. I am the God who gives talents. I am the God of the supernatural. So walk in the Spirit, be filled with the Spirit, and move in the Spirit. Use your voice and move those vocal gifts of tongues and interpretation of tongues. Use your voice and walk in the word of knowledge and word of wisdom. Flow in these gifts and impartation, and watch things be released. Operate in special faith and believe Me for special breakthroughs, special miracles, and unusual things. Believe Me for the unusual. Believe Me for something special.

Do not try to explain yourself as being different. Do

not try to pattern yourself after what you see. I do raise up models, and many of you do view those models and walk, to a degree, in that model. But I will do a new thing in the lives of many, and you will not be limited by what someone else has done. Do not copy or mimic what someone else has done. I make you a unique gift in My hand.

Don't be afraid. Don't jump back. Stir up your gift and do not neglect it. Your gift will not be shut down, and your voice will not be silenced because of fear and intimidation and the voice of the enemy, but they will be released. You will see those special endowments, those special Macedonian mandates and assignments, and those special miracles released on your behalf in the days to come.

PRAYER

Father, bless me as the reader of these words. Let the special graces of Romans 12 come upon me and cause me to be stirred. I know You have a Macedonia calling out to me—a place where my unique voice, gifting, abilities, talents, and anointing are key to revival and breakthrough. From the marketplace to the kingdom, Lord, I know You have called me for such a time as this.

I pray that as I may have been walking in old things that were Your will for a past season, let me not bring those old things into this new season. I receive the new, unusual, and special thing You are doing now. I proclaim Isaiah 42:9, which says, "Behold, the former things are come to pass, and new things do I declare: before they spring forth I tell you of them."

Father, release to me new, inspired thoughts. Release Your new plans and the new things for the next season. Let me walk in them even now.

Lord, let the prophetic word I have just read be released into my life today. Send confirmation and revelation that will launch me into the future. Thank You for this revelation as I seek to walk in Your plans and Your purposes for this season and for the season to come.

CHAPTER 3

ANSWERING THE CALL

S OME TIME AGO I came across a message by Pastor Sarah Morgan of Prayer Academy Global. It was an amazing message about the books in heaven God has written about each of us. It was a very prophetic word unlike any message I had ever heard anyone preach before.

In the message she said there are books in heaven concerning each one of us, and those books need to be opened and read. She went on to say that many people will look at you and read a line or a chapter from your book but never really read the whole book. Though we can't expect others to really know all about what we are called to do, this just lets us know that we have a responsibility to find out what's in our book so that we can live according to God's plan for our lives.

THE PROPHETIC PLAN FOR YOUR VOICE

To further support her ideas on this, Pastor Morgan quoted Psalm 40:7–8, where Jesus said, "Behold, I come; in the scroll of the book it is written of me. I delight to do Your will, O my God, and Your law is within my heart" (NKJV). We know this verse refers to the Word of God and the prophetic books that were written and prophesied long ago concerning Jesus' life and ministry. These verses about the book of Jesus' life indicate that He lived according to that prophetic plan, and He fulfilled it. For instance, in Luke 4, when He opened the book, He said, "The Spirit of the LORD is upon Me, because He has anointed Me to preach the gospel to the poor; He has sent Me to heal the brokenhearted, to proclaim liberty to the captives and recovery of sight to the blind, to set at liberty those who are oppressed; to proclaim the acceptable year of the LORD" (vv. 18–19, NKJV). And He closed the book.

One thing I want you to notice here is that Jesus was in the book. The book was about Him. His life was a book. Pastor Morgan mentioned the fact that each one of our lives is a book, but they are closed books that need to be opened, read, and understood. Jesus knew who He was and the will of God for His life because He found Himself in the prophetic books of the Bible. And in three and a half years He fulfilled every prophetic promise in the Book connected to His call and concerning His life. And He died on the cross according to the Book, or the Scriptures.

As Pastor Morgan continued with her message, I listened as she brought out the fact that we don't know what is in our own book because we have never read it. We've never sought God about opening our books or allowed Him to do it so He can show us His plan and purpose for our lives. So many of us are closed books. We've never been opened; we've never been read. But according to the Book of Revelation, Jesus is the One who has prevailed to open the book.

Pastor Morgan's message was one of the most amazing sermons I've ever heard. I shared it on my Facebook page. I've been preaching for forty years. I've heard many great messages, but I'd never heard a message like that concerning the fact that we are all books and we discover who we are by learning what's in our books.

Knowing what is written on the pages of your book is central to understanding how you are to impact the earth with the call and gifting that are on your life. There are a few ways you can discover it.

Prophetic ministry

Prophets and prophecy have a way of causing us to understand our calling, our purpose, and the plans of God, so I always encourage people to get good, quality prophetic ministry. It is very important for you to discover the will and plan of God. Often prophets bring confirmation. In other words, there may be something on your heart, you may be getting a glimpse of something, or you may be seeing through dreams and visions. These experiences may be God's attempt to show you pages from your book.

The right people

Sometimes your purpose comes into view because you connect to the right people. The right people can help you open your book and discover what's in it, especially when you connect with the right people who are also prophetic. They have insight concerning the plans and purposes of God for your life.

Now, all of us have the Holy Spirit, so the Spirit of God can also show you things about the assignments and plans He has for you. I don't want to imply that you have to depend on a prophet to discover everything you need to do. God can show you things. Prophets can reveal things to you and help you. They can be used by God to confirm, give you revelation, and help you to see things, but they never take the place of God.

For instance, Samuel anointed David with oil, signifying that he was to be the next king of Israel. (See 1 Samuel 16.) He did the same thing with King Saul. (See 1 Samuel 9.) So sometimes prophets do play an instrumental part in helping us to discover the plans and purposes God has for our lives.

INSPIRATION OVER DESPERATION

Years ago I read a book that made the point that in order to begin knowing the direction God wants you to go in life, you must have an inspired plan. That is important to remember as you seek to determine what God has written in the book of your life. Many people believe they should operate just on perspiration, telling themselves, "If I just work hard enough..." "If I perspire profusely, I'll have success." "If I just keep working, keep doing, I'm going to be successful."

Have you known anyone like this? Instead of operating with inspiration, they operate out of desperation.

Instead of being motivated by desperation, we need to be motivated by inspiration. God doesn't want our lives to be dictated by desperation; He wants us to have a plan, and He wants to inspire that plan. He wants to change us from the inside.

Many people have been taught to go to school, get a degree, get a job, get paid, get a retirement plan, get married, have children, die at a good old age, and go to heaven. But they never really move in inspiration.

The word *inspiration* means "God-breathed."[1] When God breathes on you, when He blows on you or inspires you to do something, His inspiration could move you to do something that impacts government, business, education, media, the arts, church, or ministry.

A lot of people never move by inspiration. God inspires them to do something, but they shut it down and never act on it. They don't move in it. They think that maybe what they are sensing is not God, especially when God inspires them to do something different from what everyone else is doing.

There's another thing people fall into—trying to live by someone else's inspiration and calling and trying to find their identity in someone else. Serving and following other people by being part of their ministries, organizations, or businesses is different from what I am talking about here. Sometimes God will inspire you to work alongside an individual. He'll inspire you to submit to a mentor or coach. He'll inspire you to work with an apostle, prophet, evangelist, pastor, or teacher. You can get an impartation from them as you are growing and maturing in the thing God has called you to do. But there are things—separate and different from anyone else—that God will also inspire you to do concerning your life.

INSPIRATION BRINGS UNDERSTANDING

Job 32:8 says, "There is a spirit in man: and the *inspiration* of the Almighty giveth them understanding" (emphasis added). The New King James Version says, "And the *breath* of the Almighty gives him understanding" (emphasis added).

This verse is saying that when God breathes on you, when He inspires you, when His Spirit moves on your spirit, it gives you understanding. You begin to understand the plan of God, the purpose of God, and the calling of God through inspiration. When God inspires you to do something, it is one of the most powerful things that can happen to you. I can hear Him saying, "Open a business, start a charity, get involved in the governmental realm, get involved in education, do something in ministry, create something, innovate something, build something."

Your calling is your pulpit. It is the place from which you will preach and bring heaven to earth. Can you see it? Your business is your pulpit. Your charity organization or position in local or national government is your pulpit. If you don't know just what God is calling you to, let Him breathe on you so you will understand what His plan is. Ask Him to reveal the pages of your life's book.

Then when the Spirit of God does breathe on you, don't quench the Holy Ghost. Let God breathe on you. You are a spirit being, and the inspiration of the Almighty gives you understanding.

COMMIT AND BE ESTABLISHED

Then there is Proverbs 16:3: "Commit thy works unto the LORD, and thy thoughts shall be established." In other words, commit your works, your plans, and the things you are doing to the Lord, and your thoughts shall be established.

Now, I want you to see the connection here. It basically says that when you commit what you are doing to the Lord, something happens in your thought life, your mind. This is key because we are governed or steered in a direction based on our thoughts.

In the classic edition of the Amplified Bible, Proverbs 16:3

says this: "Roll your works upon the Lord [commit and trust them wholly to Him; He will cause your thoughts to become agreeable to His will, and] so shall your plans be established and succeed."

In other words, when you commit your works to the Lord, He will cause your thoughts to become agreeable to His will. This is how you will know the will of God. So whatever you're doing—your plans, your future; whatever you're planning—when God inspires you to do something and you commit that to Him, you say, "Lord, here are my plans." The Scripture says write the vision and make it plain. (See Habakkuk 2:2.) So write your dream. Write what you're thinking, because sometimes we're inspired to do something, but we don't know exactly how it will be done or how we are to do it. We don't know all the details of what is to be done, so we need God to intervene in our thoughts, to cause our thoughts to become agreeable to His will. Because remember, finding your voice is finding the plan and purpose of God for your life.

"What is the will of God? What is God's plan for my life?" To gain the answers to these questions, you need your mind to come into agreement with His plans. You need God to work in you as His Word says: "It is God which worketh in you both to will and to do of his good pleasure" (Phil. 2:13). God is the one who works in you both to will *and* to do of His good pleasure. God will do that in you. God will cause your thoughts, your mind to become agreeable to His will when you commit your works and your plans to Him.

What this also means then is that anything in your plan that is not agreeable to God's will and purpose will fall by the wayside, and God will cause your thoughts to zero in on the exact thing He wants you to do. Then your plans will be established and succeed because your plans line up with His plan. Your thoughts line up with His thoughts, and your decisions line up with His plan and His purpose.

The Contemporary English Version says Proverbs 16:3 like this: "Share your plans with the LORD, and you will succeed." Then Psalm 37:5 adds more to this by saying, "Commit thy way unto the LORD; trust also in him; and he shall bring it to pass."

START WITH GOD

Now, this all seems so simple, and it really is. It's not difficult, but many believers have lost the power of it, and many believers have not fully committed to it. We do things on our own and say, "Well, God, if I need You, I'll call on You." Or, "If I get in trouble and things are not going well, I'll call on You."

No. Do it at the beginning. Submit your plan—whether it's regarding ministry, business, education, marriage, or relationships—to the Lord at the beginning, and your thoughts will be established according to His will.

God will charge and inspire your thoughts. He will breathe upon your mind, your thoughts, your plans, and your purposes. He will give you inspiration. That's how you will begin to succeed and move in God's will and plan for your life.

Now again, the Lord can use prophets to give you inspiration, because prophecy is inspired utterance. Whether or not you consider yourself a prophet, you will find that God uses you in this way. I have taught for years that every believer ought to be prophetic in the sense that we can hear God and do or say what He tells us to do or say. So it is that when the Spirit of God moves upon us, we begin to prophesy inspiration. We begin to speak by the inspiration of the Holy Ghost upon someone's life. We are giving them inspiration. All Scripture was God-breathed, or inspired by God (2 Tim. 3:16). Prophecy is the word of the Lord. When we prophesy, we are speaking the thoughts and mind of God.

When we prophesy over people, we're really imparting to them God's mind and thoughts for their lives, futures, and destinies. Prophecy is powerful, and it's all locked into inspiration. It demonstrates the power of inspiration.

YOUR GOD-INSPIRED, UNIQUE VOICE

Often God will inspire you to do something that is very unusual, something different, something that you've never really seen before because, as we discussed in the previous chapter, you are a unique individual with a unique voice and purpose. You have unique callings and talents. You will not do what everyone else does. You will do something very different, something new. God may send you out to be a pioneer in some area, but your knowing this comes by inspiration.

Moses was the first deliverer. God brought Moses into Egypt. No one else had done that before, and he brought Israel out of Egypt. His mission was inspired by God. At the burning bush he heard the voice of God.

David was the first to establish twenty-four hours of non-stop prophetic worship. No one had ever done what he did before. These are people who did things by inspiration. The Spirit of God came upon them. They were inspired to move into something new and fresh that had never been done before.

God wants you to find your voice. He wants you to find His will for your life. Too often we try to figure out what God is calling us to do, and we end up copying what we see others do. Now, there can be patterns. There can be blueprints. There can be other people you can look to as models who are doing very similar things. God can use them to coach and inspire you.

You may not be the first astronaut or the first CEO of a particular company. You may not be the first one to walk in a particular kind of ministry and do a particular kind of thing. But you may see someone who has done it similarly, and that person becomes a model who provides impartation and wisdom. But even in that, there's something unique about you.

God has given every one of us a unique combination of gifts. No two people are the same. That's why I love the idea of finding your voice and understanding how it has been designed to activate heaven on earth, because no one else has your voice. Your voice is unique. No one else can speak into a situation and bring the plans, solutions, breakthrough, victories, and strategies that you can.

Let me be clear: they can *try* to sound like you. People try to imitate other people's voices all the time. But a voice is like a fingerprint. Your fingerprint is unique. There are about seven billion people on the planet, and God is so amazing that He gave every one of them a unique voice.

No two people are exactly the same. Your voice is unique; it's unlike anyone else's. That shows us that God has given you abilities, talents, and gifts in a way that is unique from the way they have been given to anyone else. We can have similar gifts and talents, but the unique mix of our gifts distinguishes us from others.

You're unique, and you have a unique voice. Finding your

voice, that unique thing about you, comes through inspiration. Again, you can have people you look to as role models. You can be attracted to certain people and their gifts or expertise. They can teach you and help you much like a master would teach his or her apprentice. You may sit under someone to learn what he or she knows, but there's still something unique God has given you to do.

REFINING YOUR VOICE

Embracing something new or knowing what to do with the very unique anointing God has given can be very difficult for some people because it takes faith to step out in things like this. It takes faith to believe God and act on inspiration. It takes faith to move forward. Sometimes it takes confirmation to know what you're hearing really is from God. Having prophetic people in your corner can help with this. They will prophesy things like "You've been thinking about this...," "You've been saying this...," "You've been doing this...," or "You've been wondering what this means." Then they may confirm your thoughts by saying, "But what the Lord was saying to you is, 'It is Me. I am pushing you.'" Their words will give you confirmation.

We all struggle sometimes with what God is telling us, especially when it is so different and unique. We don't want to mess up. We don't want to do something God is not calling us to do, even if we are having visions about it.

Getting around people who inspire you is important if you're going to find your voice. This goes beyond just prophetic and religious folk. People who are doing things similar to what you do can help you refine how you use your voice. They've been there. They know what people need or expect. They can help you then go beyond that and expand into new things in the area God has called you to. When you keep company with people who inspire, they speak into who you are and where you are gifted. When they speak, breath comes out. That's the power. That's inspiration. Jesus said, "The words that I speak unto you, they are spirit, and they are life" (John 6:63). They are breath. Often God uses these individuals to speak His words to us, to breathe on us. The Greek word translated "spirit" means "breath," "wind," and "air."[2]

What's important to note here is that words carry a spirit. When someone is preaching, prophesying, decreeing, encouraging, edifying, or uplifting, their words carry the Spirit of God. Or they can carry a demonic spirit. People who lie, gossip, curse, and operate in witchcraft release demonic things with their words, their breath, their mouths. The Gospel of John says Jesus breathed on His disciples and said, "Receive ye the Holy Ghost" (John 20:22).

As you begin to refine the way God has designed you to activate heaven with your voice and your unique talents and gifts, realize that what you speak carries the Spirit of God. This will happen as long as you commit your way to Him and speak what He says to speak and do what He says to do. Your tongue must be tamed by the Holy Spirit.

The Book of James says:

> But the tongue can no man tame; it is an unruly evil, full of deadly poison. Therewith bless we God, even the Father; and therewith curse we men, which are made after the similitude of God. Out of the same mouth proceedeth blessing and cursing. My brethren, these things ought not so to be.
>
> Doth a fountain send forth at the same place sweet

water and bitter? Can the fig tree, my brethren, bear olive berries? either a vine, figs? so can no fountain both yield salt water and fresh.

Who is a wise man and endued with knowledge among you? let him shew out of a good conversation his works with meekness of wisdom.

—JAMES 3:8–13

Whether you are speaking or listening, the words that go out from you and come into your life ought to be words that are God-breathed.

When you get around people who inspire you with their words, they give you inspiration. They preach to you. They prophesy over you. Whether they are apostles, prophets, evangelists, pastors, or teachers, they stir you with their words. Their words inspire you to think new things, leading you to be innovative and creative.

You may say, "I never thought of that before." You may begin to write, think, and plan. You may begin doing things you've never done before. That is the essence of the power of preaching salvation to people. Even as you go out preaching through your life, you will inspire people to think in a whole new way, breaking them out of sin, shame, and bondage.

You must guard your voice and your gifting, so you cannot allow yourself to hang around people who don't inspire you or who inspire you to do the wrong thing. You don't need demonic inspiration. You need God's inspiration. The people who inspire you and help you find your voice, identity, calling, and purpose are those whom I call Cornelius connections. Others may call them divine connections. They are people you have been ordained by God to meet, certain people whom God has led into your life to speak into your life, prophesy, minister to you, and inspire you. These are the people who help refine your voice and make you better.

THE WORD OF THE LORD CONCERNING INSPIRATION

As I mentioned earlier, being in a prophetic atmosphere stirs us. You will continue to notice prayers, activations, confessions, and the word of the Lord placed throughout this book. I believe this will help sharpen and refine the accuracy of your voice and prepare you to embrace the sound your life will release into the earth. Even as I write this, I hear the Lord saying this:

> From My ministers, prophets, and apostles, I am releasing inspiration upon the magnitudes of My people. As they preach, prophesy, minister, and teach, they will begin to inspire you and stir you up, and you'll begin to think according to My will. My plans will be released to you, and I'll cause new vision and new dreams. I'll cause new things to be released upon you, for I'm causing My prophets to prophesy a new thing in this hour.
>
> You will begin to move in a new thing, for I have designed you to walk in new things. I'm releasing new things by inspiration, so get ready, for truly, you will do something new, fresh, and different. You'll create new models, you'll have new strategies, and you'll do new things. I'll give them to you in your dreams and in your thoughts. I'll show you things you've never seen before. I'll cause you to think in areas you've never thought in before.
>
> I'm breaking the limitations from your mind. I'm going to cause you to think outside of the box. I'm going to break the limitations of tradition, religion, and people

that have said you can't go beyond this area or you can only do it this way. I'm going to give new, creative models and new ways of breaking out of the box.

I'm breathing upon you. I'm causing your thoughts to be inspired by My word. I'm causing a new breath, a new wind to come upon you, even as you commit your ways to Me and commit your plans to Me.

I shall breathe upon your mind. I shall cause your thoughts to be inspired. And watch, in the days to come, as you move in inspiration, you'll discover new ways and new platforms. I'll connect you with the right people, those who inspire and stir you. I'll cause their words; their counsel; and their preaching, teaching, prophetic ministry to release a new breath and a new wind upon your thoughts.

I'm changing the way you think. You've been thinking the old way. You've thought in a box. Your thinking has been limited, but I'm breaking the limitations off of you, and you will discover that your gifts, calling, and anointing are much greater than you have been told. Even the hidden things—the hidden gifts, talents, abilities; the things you have neglected; the gifts you have not stirred up; the things you have overlooked; and the things you've not walked in because of fear, apprehension, uncertainty, and doubt—I am causing those things to spring back to life.

I'm causing My word to come to cause faith to be stirred in your heart that you might rise up and go forward, that you might do the things I'm calling you to do in this hour. And there'll be the release of new visions, new dreams, new strategies, new models, new blueprints, new buildings. New works shall come forward. You'll do these things, and some will say, "Why haven't I thought of that? Why didn't I think of that? I've never seen that before." Many will try to duplicate what you're doing, but they're not moving by inspiration. For when they try to copy what you're doing, you already will be moving on to something new.

You'll never ever be left behind. You'll never ever lag behind. You'll progress. You'll succeed.

I'll cause you to be on the cutting edge as you learn the power of inspiration and as I breathe upon your life. When they try to copy and duplicate what you're doing, it's time for something new. You'll keep moving, you'll keep progressing, and you'll keep advancing. You'll keep moving in a fresh, new thing. You'll keep discovering new plans and new purposes. You'll keep discovering what I've written in your book. I'm opening the book. I've called you to live not in the last chapter but in the present chapter, and there are more chapters to come.

You will see things concerning your life, business, plans, gifts, and talents that you've never seen before. And you'll walk in My uniqueness and in My calling. You'll no longer think it's strange, but you'll say, "God has made me this way," and I'll make you comfortable with who you are. You'll no longer walk in self-rejection, fear, confusion, low self-esteem, and thinking that you're not important or that the work you do is not important. You'll no longer subjugate your gifts and your calling. You'll no longer put it down and let it be dormant. But you'll walk in My uniqueness. You'll walk in the unique calling, gifting, and talent that I placed inside of you. I'm breathing upon you.

I'm causing your gifts, your destiny—even those gifts and callings in you that have been subdued—to be like a package that is being unwrapped like a Christmas gift decorated with a big bow. Take the gift wrap off, open the box, and look inside the gifts I've given you.

So commit your way to Me. Commit your plan to Me. Commit your will to Me. Commit your desires to Me, and I will cause My thoughts and your thoughts to become one. I will cause My thoughts to come into your mind, and you'll walk according to My plans and purposes in the days to come. It will come through inspiration—the breath and the wind of God that I am breathing and blowing upon you now.

PRAYER TO RECEIVE THE INSPIRATION OF GOD

Father, I thank You that just as each person's voice is unique, there is a unique calling and a unique gifting on my life.

Whether it's in business, service, ministry, government, media, or the arts, You are breathing on me, for I am not limited to the four walls of the church. Break me out of that mindset now in the name of Jesus. Though I commit to the house of the Lord, because that is where I receive inspiration, I know that my voice can expand beyond it into the mountains of culture.

I commit my way to You so that my thoughts become Your thoughts and my plans, Your plans. Help me to know my unique talent and gift. Help me discover my authentic voice. Let me discover what is on Your heart and what You are breathing on me to do.

As You cause my thoughts to become agreeable to Your will, so shall my plans be established and succeed.

Lord, I trust You with all my heart. I will not lean on my own understanding. In all my ways, I acknowledge You so You will direct my paths.

I repent for the times when I have failed to do that. Increase my faith to believe You will do all that You promise. Let Your inspired thoughts come into my mind and make my plans and thoughts agreeable to Your will. In Jesus' name, amen.

PRAYER PETITIONING GOD TO OPEN YOUR BOOK

Father, I pray now that You would open my book. Show me what is in my book. Open my eyes; open the chapters that I may read the sentences of my book. Lord, let my book not be closed to me anymore.

Open my book and show me the plans and purposes You have for me. I pray that I will see Your will clearly, Lord. I pray that as the book is opened, I will find my voice, my purpose, and Your plan for what You've called me to do. I will not waste my time doing things You never called me to do because I don't know my book.

Lord, I pray that I will not try to live my life out of another person's book. Let me know my assignment, commission, and mandate, whether it's in the church or marketplace. Whatever I am called to do,

Father, let me discover it. Help me see it. Open it up to me. Amen.

PRAYER FOR CORNELIUS CONNECTIONS

Father, I thank You for allowing this to be a season in my life when I am finding my voice. Thank You for bringing me to a place where I can know Your plan and Your purpose for my life. Lord, as I commit my works and plans to You afresh, forgive me for the times when I have tried to use my own wisdom and strength.

Lord, I commit my plans, ministry, business, education, gifts, and thoughts to You today. Let them be established according to Your will. Let me begin to walk in Your will. Let my gifts and talents come alive. Breathe upon my mind. Let me discover Your will, purpose, and plan for me, and let me walk in it.

Let my voice be a blessing to my generation. Let my actions contribute to this planet, to humanity. Let me be a blessing, and let me do what You've called me to do.

I put a stop to anything that comes to waste my time. I put a stop to anything that comes to take me off course. Any spirit that is assigned to block my gifts and talents, anything that has come to blind me from discovering what You've placed in me, and anything that causes my eyes to be closed to Your plan and purpose for my life, I cancel its assignment, in the name of Jesus. Any confusion and anything I'm doing that is not Your will for this season of my life, let it cease.

Lord, let me connect with the right people—those who inspire me, those who are part of my destiny, and those who even help me to live out my destiny. Let me be a part of the right team, and let me form the right team.

Father, I thank You, and I believe that even as I pray today, this day will be a day of change, a day of release, a day of discovering. Give me Your wisdom for how this is all to be done. You said wisdom is the principle thing, and I ask for wisdom.

Thank You for Your counsel. Thank You for Your Word. Thank You for insight. I give You praise. I give You glory. I give You honor for it all. In Jesus' name, amen.

CHAPTER 4

THROUGH ALL THE EARTH

Their line has gone out through all the earth,
and their words to the end of the world.
—PSALM 19:4, NKJV

A S THE LORD begins to breathe on your purpose and open the book of your life's destiny, He will begin to bring you into the place where your voice will be heard and heaven will come down. And just as there's no place in the world that can hide from the sun, moon, and stars—or the heavens—no place where God sends you will be left untouched by what you speak and demonstrate through the gifts and calling on your life. In other words, there is no place on the planet that is off limits to you. Your voice, your sound, your speech can go anywhere. The enemy and the people he uses can try to stop it, they can try to silence you and shut you down, but God has a way of getting your voice out into the nations.

Years ago I found out that my website had been blocked in China. At the time, the government was blocking any website that used the word *apostle* or *prophet*, among others, so the Chinese people could not find it. It wasn't personal. They just didn't want their people learning anything about the apostolic and prophetic because they think it is connected to a religious cult. But I'm here to let you know that they can try to shut the internet down, but God has a way of getting the voice of the believer wherever heaven is needed to touch earth—in China, Africa, Russia, and anywhere else. Just as you cannot stop the sun, moon, and stars from shining, your voice cannot be stopped. There is no place and no language that can keep your voice out when God wants to get it somewhere. Trust and believe that if God has given you something to say, He will make a way for your voice to be heard. No preacher, no denomination, no politician, and no government can stop your voice.

Say this with me aloud right now: "God wants to expand my voice."

God doesn't want you stuck in some little building, preaching, teaching, facilitating, or speaking to only ten people. Thank God for the ten, of course. Do not despise small beginnings (Zech. 4:10). But you have a voice that can go beyond those ten people. God can put your voice in a book and then get your book printed in different languages so your voice gets duplicated and distributed into various parts of the earth.

There may be those who don't like you, those whom the enemy uses to try to limit you by speaking against you, rejecting you, and refusing to give you a chance. Let me tell you, it didn't make any difference how many preachers didn't like me or didn't like what I was preaching. God put His words in my mouth and a pen in my hand and took my voice everywhere around the world He needed it to go. Why? Because I am the heavens. I'm above all this stuff—and you are too. We are not stuck down in the earthly realm spiritually.

If there's a situation that keeps coming to your mind—a situation happening to you right now or an incident from the past where someone tried to silence or stifle your voice— declare aloud right now, "You cannot stop my voice." Say, "When I speak, heaven speaks."

CONFESSING PSALM 19:4

Many years ago, we began to confess Psalm 19:4 for Crusaders Church. We began to say that our line, our reach as a local church would go into all the earth, and our words would go to the ends of the world. And we began to say there was no place on the planet where the voice of Crusaders would not be heard. That was our confession. We began to pray toward that, using Psalm 19:4. Then the Lord began to speak to me about people outside of our church like you—your line going out and your voice being heard. As I preached this, even I began to get calls to go and minister in other nations. I preached in over eighty nations, and many times, I took our ministry teams with me.

Then, around 1990, I began to write books. I have written over fifty books now. After the release of one of my first books, *Prayers That Rout Demons*, I heard a testimony about a woman from Ireland who received it. She said that she just happened to find it. She wasn't even a believer and was in an environment that was heavily involved in satanism and witchcraft. She began to pray the prayers out of that book, and supernatural things began to happen. She said her house began to shake, and demons began to leave. She eventually accepted the Lord and got delivered.

This is the power of one's voice being released. This book was all the way in Ireland while I was somewhere else in the world.

I also once had the opportunity to minister in Belfast, Ireland. I have also ministered in Dublin. When I was there preaching in the 1990s, a bomb exploded down the street from the church where I was speaking. The whole church building shook, and everyone in the service just sat listening to me preach as if nothing had happened. I was wondering, "Did anyone else hear a bomb go off?"

At that time, there was a civil war going on. When I returned to my hotel after preaching, I saw news reports that a hotel down the street from the church where I was speaking had been blown up. The people were so used to explosions and war that they didn't budge. During the conflict, many of the members of that church had been killed. Gunmen had even come to the church and shot it up.

Over the years of traveling and ministering around the world, I have found myself preaching in these crazy places. I don't go as much as I used to, but when I do, I have a great time prophesying, praying over people, and ministering to people.

As God called me and Crusaders Church to go to the nations, my books began to be translated into different languages: Spanish, French, Polish, Hindi, Swahili, Russian, and more. Because we began to confess Psalm 19:4, the word the Lord gave our church did not just stay with our church on the South Side of Chicago. It went to the ends of the earth through the written word and calls to the nations. We have become a church whose voice touches the world.

Your voice can go places you've never imagined. Your words can be heard in nations in which you never imagined your voice would be heard. It is really amazing how far your voice can go—and where it can go. The enemy tries to limit your voice by saying, "You can only say it here"; "You'll never go outside your city"; "You'll never go outside your state"; "You'll never go outside your nation."

Listen, if God has given you a special endowment in the area of music and worship and you begin to sing and write songs, believe your songs are going to be heard in places you never imagined they would be heard. Your voice is not limited to your bedroom or your shower. Your voice can be heard in whatever places He ordains. Even when friends and family tell you to shut up, that you have nothing to say, God can cause your voice to go to the ends of the earth, especially now with social media. You can just pick up a phone and be heard around the world. Your voice has the potential to reach the uttermost parts of the earth.

Don't limit your voice. Let it be heard. God has given you something to say. People in other nations need to hear it. God has put a word of deliverance in your mouth. People in other nations need deliverance. God has put a word of prophecy in your mouth. People in other nations need to hear that prophetic word. Your line, your measure, your reach can go throughout the earth, and your words can go to the end of the world.

TO THE ENDS OF THE EARTH

In addition to providing you with a new way to see your spiritual gifts and talents and your identity as the heavens, which declare the glory of God, I'm writing this book to help you break limitations off your voice, your sound, and your mouth. I'm not writing this to tell you something I'm believing. I'm writing this to tell you something I am experiencing in my own life. This truth is in the Word of God, and it applies to every believer. There is no place in the world where your voice is not heard and your impact for the kingdom will not be felt.

As I mentioned in chapter 1, Paul quoted Psalm 19:4 in Romans 10:18 in connection to the gospel being preached by the apostles in the first century. They had ministered from Jerusalem and Judea to Asia Minor and the uttermost parts of the earth. I don't believe many believers really know how effective the first-century church was in preaching the gospel, because in some circles, we've not really studied just how much they went out.

From the 120 believers in the Upper Room the gospel began to spread: Paul, being an apostle to the Gentiles, was sent out; Barnabas was sent out; Judas, Silas, Apollos, and Timothy too. These men went to many different cities such as Antioch, Corinth, Ephesus, and Philippi. Then, of course, there were others who went into Alexandria in Egypt, which is in northern Africa, and preached the gospel. The apostle Thomas went to India to preach the gospel and died there. When I went to India, my hosts took me to his tomb.

From the time of the apostles, the gospel did go out into all the known world in that one generation. The people of that time had a chance to hear the gospel and repent. As a matter of fact, in Colossians 1:23, Paul actually says this: "the gospel, which ye have heard, and which was preached to every creature which is under heaven."

Originally Jesus sent them out from Jerusalem, and as they began to preach the gospel, the Bible says in Acts 8:1 that God allowed a great persecution to come to the church, which actually forced them to scatter. (We'll talk more in chapter 7 about the persecution that can come as a result of being a voice of heaven, and how to withstand it.)

YOUR LINE IS GOING OUT

God is releasing your voice. Your line is going out. Your words are going out to places you never knew they would go, beyond where you ever imagined. Like the man from Macedonia who showed up in Paul's vision, people are going to be contacting you from places you never heard of, saying, "I heard your song." "I heard your message." "I heard your preaching." "I heard your conference." "I read your books."

They will be writing to you from places you never imagined. In some remote village somewhere, somebody with a phone or computer may find themselves connecting with you through an online conference, webinar, prayer call, or live Facebook or Instagram broadcast. They are going to hear a word that will break the power of hell off their life. God has a way of getting your voice out just as surely as the stars and sun shine. There is no place your voice cannot go.

Using the heavens as a metaphor, God is saying that just as the heavens cover the earth and there is no place that is hidden from the heavens, the preaching and teaching of the Word of God can go everywhere. No political system, dictator, or ruler; no witch or warlock can stop it from happening.

God is extending your voice. God called you so your voice could be heard. God saved you and filled you with the Holy Ghost so He could give you a voice. God drops His word in your mouth so you can speak it. Don't underestimate God. You can be unknown and post a video on social media that goes viral.

"OLD TOWN ROAD"

I did a study on a guy who had a hit song called "Old Town Road." His name is Lil Nas X. Before I looked into the phenomenon of the song, I didn't know about him. I first heard it while watching the BET Awards, which I don't usually watch. But this time, I happened to turn it on, and he was just coming out onto the stage. He's a black rapper performing a country song, and he had other black folks jamming to it. The song has gone all over the world.

So I did a little study on this guy and found that before he became well known, he was doing performances for children. He was going to schools performing "Old Town Road" for kids. One thing he must have known is that if you get the kids, you can get the adults. Then I read how he began to push the song on social media, and it just exploded to number one.

If a song like that can go around the world, anybody can use their creativity and produce something that could go viral. And for you, who are declaring the glory of God, remember that with God all things are possible. Don't limit Him, and don't try to figure out how He is going to perform His Word.

You may be one whom God sends to other nations. Because there is something unique in your voice that needs to be heard, He may send you to Europe, Africa, Asia, the Caribbean, Latin America, or Australia. God will open those doors for you. "Get ready," says the Lord, "You're going to find yourself speaking to people you never dreamed you would speak to."

LOCAL OR GLOBAL?

Recently a member of my church told me about a door the Lord opened for her to go to the United Nations. While there, she heard about plans for smart cities that are now being developed around the world.[1] No one lives in these cities yet, though historically, cities were built as people came to them to settle in an area.

Chicago, the city I live in, began as a fort. It was founded by a Haitian man named Jean-Baptist-Point Du Sable. He was a fur and grain trader. With all its rivers and lakes, Chicago was a significant trading post. Soon more people started moving to it, and it grew and developed into one of America's major cities. But now, according to the woman who attends Crusaders, they're building these smart cities in Africa and China in which no one yet lives. They are planned cities, and people would have to be invited to live in them.

"I feel a calling to this," she said to me. "This is different. I'm different."

What I know of her as a member of my church is that she has a call to preach and minister, but then she also felt a calling to be a part of the United Nations.

I encouraged her and said, "You're very unique. Not everyone in the church has a desire to do that, but you do, and it's important."

So she went and began to operate in this field. Her calling was something different, something unique, and something outside what we normally see within the church.

You have a voice and a call as well. It may be different. It may be unique. It may be something others don't engage in. It could be a ministry in the church. It could be something outside the church connected to government or economics.

Rapper/singer Akon is building a cryptocurrency city in Senegal.[2] It's amazing what God will do through us to bring heaven down to earth and into people's lives. Even through ventures like Akon's, which is being carried out in a place where poverty has been like hell on earth for some, great breakthrough and wealth are coming.

Remember, whatever you do—your gift, your calling—has to be committed to God.

BE THE ANSWER

While not everyone is called to be a major voice around the world, it is not your destiny to just live an ordinary life and then go to heaven one day. Your sphere of influence may not be as extensive as someone else's, but don't compare yourself to them. Doing what God has called *you* to do is important. Your gift and your calling will bring progress and blessing to humanity. You will leave a legacy and contribute something that makes life better for someone.

Recently I was teaching on one of the things God has called us to do, which is to be an answer to a problem. When we bring the voice of heaven into a situation, we bring a solution to a problem. There is always a problem that needs to be solved.

A research group called the Union of International Associations has published what is called *The Encyclopedia of World Problems and Human Potential*.[3] It is available online. As I scrolled through it, I was amazed at what are catalogued as problems on this planet. From terrorism and sanitation to poverty, women's issues, and sexual trafficking, they've listed thousands of problems in need of solutions.

God has equipped someone with a gift and a talent to bring a solution to some problem, whether it's inventing a new technology, devising a plan, or outlining a purpose. Just looking at the list of world problems, I was overwhelmed. I didn't even read them all. There were so many—ignorance, women's rights, orphans, diseases, mental health issues, drug addiction. These are all problems that need solutions, and you may have a gift that brings that solution. People need your gift, talent, and ability. As you pursue ways to solve some of the problems in our world, God will open opportunities to you and will give you a strategy as to how you can bring solutions.

You could start by developing something small—a ministry, business, charity, or organization—or even just work with someone or a company because they solve a certain problem. Fast food came about because people had a problem: they couldn't get food quickly. Fewer and fewer people had time to go home and cook three meals a day, but they had to eat. Then fast food franchises popped up everywhere, because someone figured out a way to get people food fast instead of them having to cook three meals a day at home.

But then another problem surfaced. With so many fast-food restaurants having cheap, easy, but fatty foods, people began to have health issues. This put another group of people with related gifts and talents to work on finding solutions for that.

There's always a solution to a problem.

Henry Ford invented a car because it took too long to get from point A to point B. He got rich from solving that problem. Today we have all these mobile devices because we had a problem communicating with people. We communicated, but the communication was slow or inconvenient. Thank God we don't have to use Morse code or smoke signals to communicate with people anymore. Now I can go online and talk with you through Zoom broadcasts and Facebook Live. There was a problem—lack of communication or slow communication—and someone used their ability to solve it. All these efforts made our lives better and easier, giving us the ability to do things we've never done before.

When you bring answers and solutions that make life better, you bring heaven. There is no place your voice will not go, because you have something people need. I declare that there will be no limitation to where you will go and what doors will be opened to you. If you are destined for the halls of academia, let your voice be heard in the universities. If you are destined to govern and legislate, let your voice be heard in the halls of Congress. If you are called to illuminate and enlighten the next generation, let your voice be heard in the schools and educational system.

If you are called to be an influence in media and entertainment, let your voice be heard on television and radio. Let it be heard on social media. Let it be heard in Hollywood. Let it be heard in the entertainment industry. Let it be heard everywhere. Let it be heard in the islands of the sea. Let it be heard in every nation and every language. Let the muzzle come off your mouth that you may be heard and the whole earth be blessed.

PRAYERS TO EXPAND YOUR VOICE

Father, I break any limitation that the enemy has put around my voice, in the name of Jesus.

_____

I break every power of witches and warlocks that try to stop my voice from being heard in the nations. I rebuke it.

_____

I bind demons of Islam, Communism, and humanism that say the voice of the church will not be heard. I decree Psalm 19:4 over my life.

_____

Father, release my voice wherever it needs to go. Let my voice be heard. Let my voice bring healing. Let my voice bring deliverance. Let my voice bring blessing.

_____

I decree that there is no place my voice cannot be heard. My line is being extended. My measure is being increased. When I speak, heaven is speaking. My voice is the voice of heaven. My song is the song of heaven. My prophetic word is a word from heaven.

Thank You, Lord, for causing my voice to go out to be a blessing to people I've never met or seen before—people in different nations who speak languages different from mine.

My voice will declare the glory of God. With my voice I will praise the Lord. I will rejoice.

My voice will be released in the months to come. It will go places it's never been before.

I believe my line is being extended. It's going further. It's going wide. It's going out.

There is no place, no language, no speech where my voice, the voice of the church, the gospel, and the good news will not be heard.

Lord, let the voice of the church be heard again in my land.

Let the voice of the apostle, the voice of the prophet, the voice of the evangelists, the voice of the pastor, the voice of the teacher, the voice of the psalmist be heard in every nation, city, region, neighborhood, and house, in the name of Jesus.

I will lift up my voice like a trumpet in Zion.

_____

I will let my voice be heard.

_____

I will not be afraid to release my voice.

_____

I have a fearless voice.

_____

I will say what God tells me to say.

_____

I will speak what God tells me to speak.

_____

I will decree what God tells me to decree.

_____

I will lift up my voice.

I will shout, and the walls of Jericho will come down.

I will lift up my voice like a trumpet and release heaven on earth.

Let heaven be heard, in the name of Jesus.

CHAPTER 5

HEAVENLY MINDED, EARTHLY GOOD

*If then you were raised with Christ, seek those
things which are above, where Christ is, sitting
at the right hand of God. Set your mind on
things above, not on things on the earth.*
—COLOSSIANS 3:1–2, NKJV

WHEN GOD CREATED the sun and moon, the act was more than something physical. In setting the sun to rule by day and the moon to rule by night, God established a prophetic picture of the kingdom. We should be ruling by day. We should be ruling by night. We should have authority. We should walk in the power of the kingdom. So it was not just a celestial thing when He formed the stars. It was a prophetic thing.

In 1 Corinthians 15:41, Paul talks about the glory of the stars and other celestial bodies: "There is one glory of the sun, another glory of the moon, and another glory of the stars; for one star differs from another star in glory" (NKJV). But we are the heavens who declare the glory of God. We are carriers of His glory.

Every time you look at the heavens, you ought to see yourself. You ought to see pictures of what you should be. You should see yourself shining bright, the light of the world, full of glory, full of power, and full of splendor. You are not just anybody, though the devil will try to make you think you are. He will beat you down and beat you up. The lies he tells you will cause you to hang your head low if you don't have a revelation about your heavenly identity.

Coming to understand who you are in these new terms may be easier said than done. As you are reading this, you may be saying, "I don't feel like the heavens." We are not talking about feelings. We are talking about faith. Get out of your feelings. This is about faith and what the Word of God says. You must confess this—"I am the heavens"—even though you don't feel like it. You may feel like a total loser, but you'd better start opening your mouth and confessing what God says about you.

Come out of self-pity. You don't have to be a victim. You are not a loser. Begin to say what God says. The devil is a liar. God is about to do something new in your life, and it's going to come by revelation and insight in the Word of God. You are so much bigger than you realize. God is trying to show us in Scripture that He created us to live higher than the things of this earth. Don't live below your status. You are the heavens.

THE THINGS ABOVE

You've probably heard people say, "You're so heavenly minded, you're no earthly good." I don't believe that. If you are truly heavenly minded, you do a lot of good on the earth. The problem is that we don't have enough heavenly minded people. Instead, many are carnal and earthly. You need to be heavenly minded, which is to be spiritually minded. You need to manifest the heavens on the earth. What is in heaven? Glory, power, and authority. There is no poverty in heaven. There is no lack in heaven. There is no sickness in heaven. And it is possible to have a touch of heaven while you are on earth. Don't settle with hell on earth. Have faith to live like heaven on earth.

The heavens rule over all. Stop looking at yourself as just some earthly person stuck on this planet. You can live above the things of earth, the things of this fallen existence. Don't let what is happening in the earth bring you down. Don't let earthly people depress you. You can set your mind on things above and live above it all.

You can praise God. You can have joy. You can speak. You can prophesy. You can pray. You can sing. You can take authority, because you are the heavens. Breakthrough happens in heaven. Healing happens in heaven. In heaven the righteousness, justice, and love of God reign. Heaven is a place where miracle after miracle after miracle takes places. In the heavens, miracles are normal.

As your mind is set on things above, you speak as heaven speaks. The Bible says, "As [a man] thinks in his heart, so is he" (Prov. 23:7, NKJV). Think on the things of heaven. Think miracles. Think prosperity, deliverance, and shalom.

God is expanding your voice. Your line is going throughout the earth. Everywhere it goes, your voice activates the miraculous. Your voice changes lives and sets free those who are held captive by the enemy. "Whatsoever things are true,"

Philippians 4:8 says, "whatsoever things are honest, whatsoever things are just, whatsoever things are pure, whatsoever things are lovely, whatsoever things are of good report; if there be any virtue, and if there be any praise, think on these things." These are the things that exist in heaven. These are the things, as voices of heaven, we walk in. Be heavenly minded *and* be of great good in the earth.

RELEASING THE MIRACULOUS

Your voice releases the goodness of God into the earth. Those under the sound of your voice will be changed, healed, and delivered. We've discussed your line being connected to your voice and how God has gifted you in unique ways to spread the gospel—through preaching, teaching, writing books and songs, solving problems, and making the world better. Your gifts are essential to how you will uniquely activate heaven and loose on earth what is loosed in heaven (Matt. 18:18).

In 2 Timothy 1:6–7, Paul told Timothy to stir up the gift of God that was in him. As we have discussed, another word for *gift* is *endowment*. Paul told Timothy to stir up the special endowment God had given him by prophecy with the laying on of hands. He went on to tell him not to neglect the gift God had given him.

What I've discovered is that God is not limited in what He bestows upon us in the area of gifts and talents. There are more than just the twelve manifestations of the Spirit found in Romans 12 and 1 Corinthians 12. There is more He can fill us with than the fivefold ministry in Ephesians 4. Endowments are more than just those gifts.

Often when you get baptized in the Holy Spirit, God will reveal how He has gifted you in a dream or in a church service. He may speak to you by prophecy with the laying on of hands. He may give them to you through an encounter with His glory. He may also just impart special endowments, gifts, abilities, and talents into your life as you grow and develop.

Every Spirit-filled believer has one special gift. Some have more than one. These special endowments lead to miraculous results. The Amplified Bible even uses the term *special endowments* to describe the gifts given to us, which release miraculous or supernatural power: "Now about the spiritual gifts [the special endowments given by the Holy Spirit], brothers and sisters, I do not want you to be uninformed" (1 Cor. 12:1, AMP).

What can be released through writing, which is not one of the spiritual gifts listed in the Bible, is very important, because when you have an endowment to write, your books can touch people around the world, as I have shown. The woman who was delivered through *Prayers That Rout Demons* wasn't a believer. She had not been previously introduced to my books. She just happened upon one. To this day I don't know how she got the book. I've never ministered to her, but she got delivered through one of my books.

As you begin to explore how God wants to expand and release your voice, you must also stir up the endowments He's imparted to you and move in them because they can bring heaven—deliverance, miracles, and supernatural results—into people's lives. Don't allow anyone to shut down your gift and calling. Connect with apostles, prophetic leaders, and pastors who are willing to help groom you, stir you up, and release you instead of trying to shut you down or control you. Connect with leaders who will promote you and push you.

Within the realm of my apostolic calling I have an anointing or special endowment to stir people, to challenge and promote them. God has given me many sons and daughters around the world. There are many leaders who do not share their platforms with anyone, especially if they're just starting out. They wait until the person becomes well known before they invite them to their ministry. I'm not that way. It is part of my apostolic vision to promote and stir up others. As Paul did with Timothy and Moses with Joshua, part of my apostolic endowment is to raise up sons and daughters and to help release and activate them. And for many of them, my calling is to release them into the area of special endowments.

If you follow me on social media, then you may have noticed how I use my platforms to highlight other gifts. I feel a release to do this because I want to help people walk in the destiny, purpose, and calling of God that will expand the reach of their voices.

My prayer is that this book will be another way I can reach so many more sons and daughters of God whom I can't touch personally. This is part of my special endowment that releases others into their gifts and, even further, to walk in the level of special endowments.

SPECIAL ENDOWMENTS FUELED BY SPECIAL FAITH LEAD TO SPECIAL MIRACLES

First Corinthians 12:8–10 lists some of the special gifts of the Spirit: "to one is given by the Spirit the word of wisdom; to another the word of knowledge by the same Spirit; to another faith by the same Spirit; to another the gifts of healing by the same Spirit; to another the working of miracles; to another prophecy; to another discerning of spirits; to another divers kinds of tongues; to another the interpretation of tongues." But then verse 28 says, "And God hath set some in the church, first apostles, secondarily prophets, thirdly teachers, after that miracles, then gifts of healings, helps, governments, diversities of tongues." This is where God establishes a distinction in the level of gifting and raises it to *special* gifts and *special* endowments. Let's start with healing.

Healing

There are special endowments of healing. We know that all of us can lay hands on the sick. All of us can heal. Jesus said of all those who believe, "They shall lay hands on the sick, and they shall recover" (Mark 16:18). But then there are also gifts of healings, special endowments that give people a greater ability to heal, especially in difficult cases like cancer, diabetes, or rare diseases.

This is a special endowment we really need because there are so many sicknesses and diseases that sometimes are difficult to overcome, especially cancer. But I believe there is a special endowment to heal cancer. I know people who have been healed of cancer supernaturally through these special endowments.

Miracles

Then there is the special endowment of miracles. All of us can operate in miracles. Deliverance is a miracle ministry. I believe there are special endowments for deliverance. But then there is the actual working of miracles. First Corinthians 12:28 says, "And God has appointed these in the church: first apostles, second prophets, third teachers, after that miracles" (NKJV). Miracles are a ministry. Being able to flow in this level of ministry means you have a special endowment.

In Acts 19:11–12, we see that God worked special miracles by the hands of Paul.

Tongues

There are special endowments of tongues. Again, all of us can speak in tongues as a result of being baptized in the Holy Spirit. But then there is the gift of diversities of tongues, which gives you the ability to speak in tongues on a different level. This endowment can operate in intercession, in inter-pretation of tongues, or in speaking different languages. It is a different level of anointing. When you pray, sing, or minister in tongues, very supernatural things can happen. According to 1 Corinthians 14:22, tongues are a sign to unbelievers that can actually convict them and let them know that God is real.

In the days of the Azusa Street Revival, the endowment of tongues was so strong that when many of the people were baptized in the Holy Spirit, God gave them the supernatural ability to speak a foreign language. They went to countries where that language was spoken and actually preached and understood that language. We can see the precedent for this set with the apostles after Pentecost.

> And they were all filled with the Holy Ghost, and began to speak with other tongues, as the Spirit gave them utter-ance. And there were dwelling at Jerusalem Jews, devout men, out of every nation under heaven.
>
> Now when this was noised abroad, the multitude came together, and were confounded, because that every man heard them speak in his own language.
>
> And they were all amazed and marvelled, saying one to another, Behold, are not all these which speak Galilaeans? And how hear we every man in our own tongue, wherein we were born? Parthians, and Medes, and Elamites,

and the dwellers in Mesopotamia, and in Judaea, and Cappadocia, in Pontus, and Asia, Phrygia, and Pamphylia, in Egypt, and in the parts of Libya about Cyrene, and strangers of Rome, Jews and proselytes, Cretes and Arabians, we do hear them speak in our tongues the wonderful works of God.

—Acts 2:4–11

I know of one person to whom God gave the supernatural ability to speak French. She is a Spanish-speaking woman of God who also speaks English, but she learned French supernaturally. She now speaks and understands it, though she never studied it. That is a special endowment. Most of us have to learn a language, but she just received the ability. Now she speaks three languages: French, Spanish, and English.

Faith

I love this next endowment: special faith, or the gift of faith. Romans 12:3 tells us that God gives every person a measure of faith. Special faith, however, gives certain people the ability to believe God for unusual things. It is a level of faith that causes a person to believe God for ridiculous things. I love this gift because it really opens up the miracle realm and gives people the ability to believe God for supernatural things.

Knowledge

The special endowment of knowledge is one that God gave to Daniel and the three Hebrew boys. There is both the spirit of knowledge and the word of knowledge, which is another endowment where you receive knowledge of a particular event, a person, or a situation—past, present, or future. This endowment gives you the ability to know things supernaturally. All of us should have knowledge. All of us should study. But there's a spiritual endowment of knowledge where you just know things of God on a different level.

Wisdom

One of my favorite endowments is wisdom. Wisdom is the principle thing we all should have. The Bible says in all your getting, get wisdom (Prov. 4:7). Christ is your wisdom (1 Cor. 1:30). If you lack wisdom, ask God for it (Jas. 1:5–6). God gave Solomon a special endowment of wisdom through a dream (1 Kings 3). He received unusual wisdom greater than any king in history. No king before him or after him had the level of wisdom God had given Solomon.

Joshua received an endowment of wisdom when Moses laid his hands on him (Deut. 34:9). The Bible says Joshua was filled with the spirit of wisdom.

Churches can have an endowment of special wisdom. Paul prayed for the Ephesian church to be filled with the spirit of wisdom and revelation (Eph. 1:17). Even as Paul prayed for the church to have a wisdom, knowledge, and understanding of the will of God, he also had a revelatory endowment. He had special revelation and insight into the plans and purposes of God above the apostles of his day. In his letters to the first-century church Paul wrote about these mysteries. He also wrote about understanding, which is also an endowment that allows people to not only know the mysteries of God—the deeper things of God—but also to understand them.

These endowments of wisdom, knowledge, understanding, and revelation are what lead us to know God and the mysteries of the kingdom in deeper ways. I love this endowment because it really gives people, preachers, ministers, and believers a special ability to unlock certain things in

Scripture, to see things in the Bible beyond the normal interpretation or what's on the surface.

Discernment

Then there's a special endowment of discernment, which is also called discerning of spirits. This endowment gives you the ability to see things other people don't see, to discern the spirit or intent behind an action or behavior—the motive. It enables you to distinguish between what is heavenly and what is earthly, or what is angelic, demonic, or human. It helps you know when God's Spirit is moving and when you're seeing just a manifestation of the flesh. Discernment is a special endowment all of us should desire. It is also connected to wisdom. All of us should have some measure of discernment, but some of us have a special endowment of discernment, such as those in the office of a prophet or who have a strong prophetic gift.

Mercy

Romans 12 talks about the gift of mercy. It is a special endowment of compassion. It could be compassion for hurting people, homeless people, people who are in trouble. While I will continue to say that as believers we should all have a measure of the gifts I am discussing, there is a special endowment given to some that when they operate in the area of their unique and specific gifting, the supernatural, the miraculous becomes evident.

The gift of mercy and compassion is what drove Jesus to perform miracles among the crowds of people who followed Him. The Bible said He "was moved with compassion toward them, and he healed their sick" (Matt. 14:13–14). In Matthew 20:30–34, two blind men were sitting by the roadside, "and when they heard that Jesus was going by, they shouted, 'Lord, Son of David, have mercy on us!' The crowd rebuked them and told them to be quiet, but they shouted all the louder, 'Lord, Son of David, have mercy on us!' Jesus stopped and called them. 'What do you want me to do for you?' he asked. 'Lord,' they answered, 'we want our sight.' Jesus had compassion on them and touched their eyes. Immediately they received their sight and followed him" (NIV).

Jesus walked in the miraculous and released all kinds of special miracles that showed the heart of His Father toward mankind. He unlocked the miracles of heaven in people's lives because He has special endowments of mercy, compassion, miracles, faith, healing, and many more. Jesus is our example of what it looks like to fully operate in the supernatural power of God. Through His earthly ministry He showed what it looks like to release heaven on earth.

> When Jesus landed and saw a large crowd, he had compassion on them, because they were like sheep without a shepherd. So he began teaching them many things.
> —MARK 6:34, NIV

Do you feel a strong sense of compassion when you see the suffering of others, when you see their hurt and brokenness? Does it cause you to act on their behalf without giving thought about what you will receive in return? Is your focus on relieving their burdens? You may have the gift of special mercy. This is an endowment that really leaves supernatural results when you operate in it.

Giving

The special endowment of giving empowers people with the ability to give in unusual, supernatural ways. All of us should give. All of us should sow. But there are givers and people who can sow large amounts of money, extreme givers whose giving actually releases miracles. I've been at conferences where one person who has this gift paid off the whole conference. I've led conferences where we received offerings that took care of the whole conference budget. All expenses were paid by the few who were endowed with special giving.

We need to believe God for special endowments like this. Pastors should not be struggling with budgets and struggling with trying to raise offerings when these endowments are in the body of Christ.

There were women in Jesus' ministry and in the ministry of the apostles who had endowments of giving. "Certain women," Luke 8:2–3 says, "which had been healed of evil spirits and infirmities, Mary called Magdalene, out of whom went seven devils, and Joanna the wife of Chuza Herod's steward, and Susanna, and many others, which ministered unto him of their substance." The word *substance* here means "possessions, goods, wealth, property."[1] Lydia (Acts 16) and Phoebe (Romans 16) in the early church were women of influence and wealth who were patrons and benefactors for Paul's ministry.

Gifts such as this one open up opportunities to ministries and keeps them from being limited by finances. As the kingdom expands, this gift is a more and more important one. You never know who has been given an impartation of extreme giving, but if we open up to this endowment, we will see supernatural results.

Exhortation/encouragement

To exhort and encourage someone out of complacency, defeat, self-doubt, and pity into action, faith, and prosperity is a special endowment. A person with this gift not only moves individuals but also organizations. They are the kind who start movements that instigate ripple effects of change that ultimately can change the world. This gift is connected to a prophetic endowment, because if you remember, the basis of prophetic ministry is this: "he who prophesies speaks edification and exhortation and comfort to men" (1 Cor. 14:3, NKJV).

Some preachers have this endowment. When they preach, you just get encouraged. When those with this gift teach, you get encouraged. They have a special endowment to encourage people.

Some people actually complain that the prophetic ministry of some is too sugary, that they speak too well of things. They would rather hear prophecies of judgment and rebuke. But I like what one leader said in response to this. He said encouragement is lacking in the church.

How can there be too much encouragement? If anything, in some places there is too little encouragement. Is it possible to be overencouraged? Of course there is a place for prophecies that correct and rebuke. But we need to be encouraged.

This gift has been connected with the apostle Barnabas. He was called the "son of encouragement" (Acts 4:36, NIV). You may have a gift to exhort people, especially the hurting, bruised, afflicted, and discouraged. Exhortation is a special endowment. All of us should exhort and encourage people, but there is a special gift for it that activates supernatural release and breakthrough.

Service/helps

Serving others, also known as the gift of helps, is another endowment found in Romans 12. People with this special endowment assist, help, and serve men and women of God, bringing relief and uplifting the arms of others. Elisha poured water on the hands of Elijah. Aaron and Hur lifted up the hands of Moses. We call this supportive ministry. Other expressions of this endowment in the church are ushers, greeters, and administrative people. This gift extends into the marketplace as well. Administrative, executive, and personal assistants; operations officers; and so on can also fit within the expressions of this endowment.

If you are gifted with the gift of service and help, you bring great blessing to the leadership of your church, group, or organization. You really help them to fulfill the call and mandate on their lives.

Prophecy

This endowment gives you a greater ability to move in the prophetic. Every believer should be activated in the area of prophecy. We should all "covet to prophesy" (1 Cor. 14:39), and when we are baptized in the Holy Ghost, we can all move in the realm of the prophetic. But there is a special endowment of the prophetic. It can operate in singing—a psalmist, for example. It can operate in preaching, teaching, personal prophecy, corporate prophecy, and intercession. Prophecy brings the mind and heart of God into the earth realm, releasing supernatural results. Great breakthroughs and miracles happen when we operate in these special endowments.

Counsel

Being able to give people the right counsel, wisdom, and advice is a special gift and endowment. It's known as having a spirit of counsel. From time to time, any one of us can give a good piece of advice. God, Jesus, and the Holy Spirit can give us counsel, and we can share it with others as we've learned things through our own life experiences. But then there are people who have a special grace, ability, talent, and endowment to counsel. We need them, because in a multitude of counselors, there is safety.

Some people need counseling before they make a mistake. Sometimes people get their lives all messed up, then they go for counseling. But counseling is not only for after you mess up. If you seek wise counsel before you take an action or move into another season of life, it will help you prevent mistakes. It will give you advice before you mess up, give you strategy about your life and your future. Preventive counseling is like having a coach who will walk with you through the journey, helping light the path ahead of you and helping you know what is God's will for your life.

Singing

There are singing endowments. In some circles we call those with this gift psalmists. David, Chenaniah, Asaph, Heman, and Jeduthun had this endowment (1 Chron. 15:22; 25:1–9). This not only included prophetic singing but also minstrel or musical endowments. For instance, David was gifted with the harp. He was a cunning player of the harp.

You can be supernaturally endowed in the area of music. Gospel music legend Andraé Crouch supernaturally learned how to play the piano. In 1952, when Andraé was a young boy, his father prayed that God would teach his son to play the piano. He was a pastor of a small church that had no musicians. One Sunday, Andraé's father told his son to go sit at the piano. All of a sudden, Andraé just began to play. He had never taken lessons, and before that moment, he had never played the piano. He said, "Somehow I found the tonic note, and my ears just popped open. I started playing, just like that, with both hands! Then the little songs began to come...and they never stopped!"[2]

In the years after that supernatural impartation, Andraé Crouch became one of the premier musical talents in the world. The gift to play the piano was just given to him by God. He went on to write many songs.

Musical, singing psalmist and minstrel endowments are needed in the church because we need people who don't just sing but also open the heavens when they sing. Miracles and breakthroughs occur because they lift their voices or play their instruments using this endowment.

Preaching

I love both teaching and preaching endowments, but I really love good preaching. There are some whom God gives the ability to preach and teach in ways that release the supernatural. Paul had a preaching and teaching endowment. Apollos is another apostle from the early church whom the Bible says was mighty in the Scriptures (Acts 18:24, NKJV). He had a strong preaching endowment. Jesus was also anointed by God to preach the gospel (Luke 4:18).

Revelation

Also known as the spirit of revelation, there is a revelatory endowment. Paul had this endowment to understand the deeper and mysterious things of God, as was mentioned previously. These kinds of endowments are given to the church, and we need revelatory endowments in order to move forward in revelation.

Some churches and ministries just have a higher degree of revelation, which can be seen in how they study and divide the Word. It can also come through prayer.

Power and might

There is a spirit of might (*chayil*), the spirit whereby you can operate in levels of power that produce miracles and healing as well as powerful preaching, teaching, and services. We will look at how this connects to character and virtue in the next chapter. For now, remember that power and virtue must operate together to create a righteous and godly balance.

When someone with the special endowment of might or power ministers, people feel they have just come into contact with the power of God.

Wealth and finance

Deuteronomy 8:18 says, "For it is He who gives you power to get wealth, that He may establish His covenant which He swore to your fathers, as it is this day" (NKJV). There are endowments for building businesses and wealth. There are endowments for fundraising and philanthropy. I know preachers and ministers who have a special endowment to raise offerings. They have a grace in this area, and it is not just to get money. They know how to stir people to give so they can receive miracles. They know how to raise the level of giving so budgets are met.

The Bible says wealth, riches, and joy are gifts of God (Eccles. 5:19–20), so don't feel any shame in walking fully in this endowment if this is the area in which God has gifted you. The church has a ways to go in understanding blessing, wealth, and financial prosperity.

Prayer

Some people just have a gift of prayer. They have a calling to pray. Epaphras was one who labored fervently in prayer for the Colossian church (Col. 4:12). All of us should pray. We know this—"men always ought to pray and not lose heart," Jesus told us in Luke 18:1 (NKJV). The church, of course, should pray, but there are special endowments of prayer given to prophets, intercessors, special prayer ministries, and those who are given special prayer callings or assignments for certain seasons. This is what identifies someone as having a special endowment of prayer.

Evangelism

While all of us should evangelize by sharing the gospel with others to win the lost, there are people with strong evangelistic or revivalistic anointings. Billy Graham, Reinhard Bonnke, and those within my networks such as Sophia Ruffin and Ryan LeStrange are great examples of those who have strong revivalistic anointings. No matter what they are preaching about, people get convicted and saved. When they preach, the backslider even comes back to the Lord.

Pastoring

Pastors, bishops, overseers, and apostolic overseers, who have the ability to shepherd and watch over people to teach and train them, have shepherding or pastoral endowments.

Pioneering

The pioneering endowment expresses itself in those who plant churches or blaze trails in certain industries and sectors of society. We may see this in the church, as demonstrated by apostolic mothers and fathers who raise up spiritual sons and daughters. They will charge and authorize those who are under their leadership. This is a special endowment that some people just carry. When they preach, teach, or just enter a room, their authority in this area is evident.

People were amazed at the authority Christ demonstrated when He preached and cast out devils and when He spoke to the wind and waves and they obeyed Him. "What manner of man is this?" they asked each other. (See Matthew 8:27.) Jesus was manifesting this endowment.

This pioneering, apostolic endowment is not something you can work up or just do. It is a level of authority God gives you that is often connected to the office of an apostle or prophet.

Understanding

The ability of understanding, to comprehend and unravel mysteries and decode hidden things, even the secrets of God—these are specially endowed by God for His glory. They help bring solutions to the earth and unlock the mysteries of the kingdom, which are hidden truths, so God's people can prosper and God can be glorified.

Writing

This is one endowment I truly love. Scribes, writers, and authors can operate within the endowment of writing, whereby they write and their books impact people. This is an endowment God has given me. I have an apostolic endowment. I have an endowment for revelation. These endowments are not things I asked for. They are gifts God has given me. I've received them through the baptism in the Holy Spirit, being involved in environments, and through impartation and prophecy with the laying on of hands, all at certain times in my ministry. I love the endowment of writing because it changes lives.

This writing endowment is very important because there are some things that writing can do that other things cannot do. God has always appointed and used writers to help people read, connect, and understand Him, His ways, and His will for their lives. The entire Bible was written by people whom God gifted with the endowment of writing. Moses had a writing endowment. He wrote down the revelations of the Pentateuch. The prophets would have writers and scribes transcribe their writings into books and letters. Paul had an endowment to write. He wrote the letters to the churches in the New Testament. These writings are in our Bibles. These writings change history, change lives, and bring revelation.

If you have a revelatory endowment, you can write those revelations. You can give insight, understanding, and wisdom through your writing, and when people read your book, they can get activated. As you are endowed with a gift of exhortation, you can exhort and encourage people through your writing. If you have an endowment of wisdom, and you write the wise sayings and messages that God has given you, your wisdom goes out, and people get the wisdom they need to live a good life. If you have a prophetic endowment, you can write prophetically. You can write your visions and dreams.

Dreams and visions

Finally, there is an endowment for visions and dreams. Daniel had this endowment. Joseph also had this endowment. They both also had an endowment to interpret dreams.

Do you understand the dream realm? You are specially endowed in this area if you do. You may not understand fully how to operate within this area of gifting. It is special. If you develop it, if you don't neglect it, if you stir it up and connect with the right mentors and leaders who also flow in this area, you will see how it brings supernatural results, miracles, and breakthroughs into the lives of those you minister to and serve.

YOUR HEAVENLY GIFTING IS YOUR VOICE

We have covered about twenty-five of the special ways God can uniquely gift His people to bring heaven to earth. You must have the mind of God, which is indeed heavenly minded, if these gifts are to be a benefit to those you come in contact with throughout your life on earth. Don't accept it as a criticism when people say believers are of no earthly good because they are heavenly minded. The Bible says we have the mind of Christ. It says we are to imitate His life and ministry. Jesus was fully endowed by the Spirit of God in every way to show us the Father and to teach us about the kingdom.

As God begins to stir you in the area in which He has endowed you, begin by knowing you can't limit God. God can give you an unusual endowment that you haven't really seen anyone operate in before. He can gift you and someone else with the same endowment, and that endowment could be expressed in very different ways because there are diversities of gifts and endowments. There are diversities of tongues and all kinds of diverse workings of miracles. Look up the words *divers* and *diversity* as they are used in the Bible. There are differences of administrations, differences of operation. You can't put two people in the same box. Depending on the gift mix, one's endowment may operate in a very different way from another's.

As God opens your life to His wonders, and as He expands your voice and influence in the earth, continue to study special endowments and how to operate in the special assignments, commissions, mandates, talents, abilities, and gifts that He imparts to you and others. The special miracles, breakthroughs, and supernatural things God is able to do are exceedingly abundantly above all that we ask or think. There are so many gifts. All of us have some of these things, and in an apostolic environment these gifts are imparted, activated, stirred up, stretched, and launched. It is amazing how God releases these heavenly gifts to us to enrich our lives and the lives of those we are assigned to impact.

Pursue the gifts. God does not want you lacking in these endowments. All of them are supernatural and special. They result in supernatural breakthroughs and miracles. As we went through these endowments, perhaps you found yourself saying, "I have that one," but you've neglected it. I challenge you to stir it up. You can be reactivated through prophetic impartation and the laying on of hands. This is why it is so important that you remain connected in a good, prophetic church that has leaders who love to see people prosper.

This is God's heart for you. He wants you to have an abundance of gifts. He doesn't want you to shut Him down because of fear, religion, or tradition. He doesn't want witches and witchcraft to shut His gifts and endowments down in your life. He doesn't want you to die never having walked in these special endowments and seeing these special things happen in your life. So pursue the gifts. Seek knowledge and training. Don't be afraid to live above, to live in the heavenly realm. That is your home. You are seated in heavenly places.

PRAYER TO ALIGN YOUR MIND AND GIFTS WITH HEAVEN

Father, I thank You for this word. I thank You for revealing to me even now all the special gifts and endowments You have put inside of me.

Lord, even as these gifts are wrapped like a beautiful gift at Christmas, I pray that You would untie the bow and begin to unwrap the package.

Let it no longer be a package wrapped up so that I don't know what the gift is. I pray that by Your Spirit, You will open the package for me now that I may discover the gifts, talents, abilities, and unique things You've put inside of me.

As I discover them, let me also walk and move in them. Inspire my thoughts and align my mind with Your mind that I may know Your plans for me. Let me be heavenly minded that I may be of earthly good. Let all these things be revealed to me now in this season and in the days to come. In Jesus' name I pray. Amen.

CHAPTER 6

VOICE AND VIRTUE

Giving all diligence, add to your faith virtue;
and to virtue knowledge; and to knowledge
temperance; and to temperance patience; and
to patience godliness; and to godliness brotherly
kindness; and to brotherly kindness charity.

—2 PETER 1:5–7

SOME TIME AGO I'd been studying the word *chayil*. It's a Hebrew word that translates to the English word *virtuous* in Proverbs 31:10. Because this word carries so much significance and is used throughout the Old and New Testaments, I wrote a book about it called *Chayil: Release the Power of a Virtuous Woman*. We even hosted a conference by the same name. As I have already written and spoken about on many occasions, the Lord dealt with me very strongly about this word *virtuous*, which means power, strength, and even moral excellence and good character.

While I had focused on the Bible translations that reflected the power-related meanings for the word, the Lord said to me,

"You cannot walk in the power aspects of the *chayil* anointing without also having virtue." By this He meant having moral excellence and good character. Then the Lord gave me a scripture from the Book of 2 Peter. The passage really shook me, because it showed He was challenging me in this area:

> Whereby are given unto us exceeding great and precious promises: that by these ye might be partakers of the divine nature, having escaped the corruption that is in the world through lust. And beside this, giving all diligence, add to your faith virtue; and to virtue knowledge; and to knowledge temperance; and to temperance patience; and to patience godliness; and to godliness brotherly kindness; and to brotherly kindness charity.
>
> —2 Peter 1:4–7

When I read this verse, the Lord said to me, "Notice the first thing I do: I tell My people to add to their faith not knowledge but virtue." Then He said this: "A lot of believers—when they get saved—have faith, but instead of virtue, the first thing they want to add to their lives is knowledge."

Whenever we come into something new—a new job; a new assignment; a new place; a new discovery about ourselves, such as a gift or personality trait; a new prophetic word—we start reading books, sign up for training or coaching, search for mentorship, or attend conferences. These are all things that give us knowledge. But we skip over virtue.

The 1828 edition of Webster's Dictionary defines *virtue* as "bravery valor," which was "the predominant signification of virtus among the Romans." It also notes that "this sense is nearly or quite obsolete." Another definition of virtue is "moral goodness; the practice of moral duties and the abstaining from vice, or a conformity of life and conversation to the moral law. In this sense, virtue may be, and in many instances must be, distinguished from religion. The practice of moral duties merely from motives of convenience, or from compulsion, or from regard to reputation, is virtue as distinct from religion. The practice of moral duties from sincere love to God and his laws, is virtue and religion."[1]

In the same vein, author and minister Art Katz says that perhaps *virtue* is "an archaic word, used in the times of the King James translators as a synonym for power, but today the word *virtue* has to do with things ethical and moral."[2] He is speaking to how the word's definition, understanding, and usage has changed over time. Like Katz, I believe the various uses of this word are "more than just an accident of time and language."[3] There is "a conjunction between virtue and power and that the amount of power for healing [and the myriad of other gifts], in us as in Him, is relative to the proportion of virtue [ethical and moral excellence] in which we walk."[4]

A virtuous life is in sync with God's holy standards. A preacher once put it like this: "Virtue is the Godly influence of a life that is in a right relationship with the Lord and filled with the power of the Holy Spirit."[5]

Synonyms for *virtue* that shed more light on it being about living according to moral and ethical standards are "character, decency, goodness, honesty, integrity, morality, probity, rectitude, righteousness, rightness, uprightness."[6]

Then when we go to the Word, we see where virtue is joined with righteousness, morality, and justice.

> For the LORD is [absolutely] righteous, He loves righteousness (virtue, morality, justice); the upright shall see His face.
>
> —PSALM 11:7, AMP

Jesus loved virtue. He was anointed with the oil of gladness because of virtue.

> You have loved righteousness (virtue, morality, justice) and hated wickedness; therefore God, your God, has anointed You above Your companions with the oil of jubilation.
>
> —PSALM 45:7, AMP

Virtue is integrity and uprightness in purpose. Lawlessness and injustice are opposite of virtue.

> You have loved righteousness [integrity, virtue, uprightness in purpose] and have hated lawlessness [injustice, sin]. Therefore God, Your God, has anointed You with the oil of gladness above Your companions.
>
> —HEBREWS 1:9, AMP

Wisdom admonishes us to hold on to the virtues of loyalty and kindness.

> Never tire of loyalty and kindness. Hold these virtues tightly. Write them deep within your heart.
>
> —PROVERBS 3:3, TLB

Paul lists virtues we should have as God's chosen people. These virtues include compassion, kindness, humility, gentleness, patience, forgiveness, and love.

> Therefore, as God's chosen people, holy and dearly loved, clothe yourselves with compassion, kindness, humility, gentleness and patience. Bear with each other and forgive one another if any of you has a grievance against someone. Forgive as the Lord forgave you. And over all

these virtues put on love, which binds them all together in perfect unity.

—COLOSSIANS 3:12–14, NIV

Having virtue is also about honesty.

My hope is in you, so may goodness [blamelessness; innocence] and honesty [virtue] guard me.

—PSALM 25:21, EXB

Those who are honest [have integrity/virtue] will live in the land, and those who are innocent [blameless] will remain in it.

—PROVERBS 2:21, EXB

Virtue gives you the ability to live a good life.

People who live good lives [walk in virtue/integrity] respect [fear] the LORD, but those who live evil lives don't [go the wrong way on their paths despise him].

—PROVERBS 14:2, EXB

So when people try to rush past the process and want to skip over cultivating the traits in life that produce good character and moral excellence, we end up with people who get a lot of knowledge but have no character to sustain the promotion God brings into their lives. In prophetic and Spirit-filled circles they may learn all about the prophetic, the apostolic, deliverance, and spiritual warfare, and in the wider church they may learn about giving, faith, and prayer, but they skip virtue. There are even many ministers who have a lot of knowledge but lack virtue.

This is dangerous and does not work when it comes to using your voice in a way that moves heaven. The main reason this doesn't work is because knowledge puffs up. Knowledge without virtue can lead to pride, and God resists the proud (Jas. 4:6). Their voices may sound good to those who are hearing with their natural ears, but in the spirit, their sound will have little effect. It will be like tinkling brass and a sounding cymbal. But it is the prayers of the righteous (or virtuous) that avail much. It is to the humble that God grants His grace. Trying to use and amplify your voice before you have obtained virtue is a fall waiting to happen.

Nowadays in some circles everybody knows about the apostolic and prophetic. You go on social media, and everyone is an apostle or prophet. Everyone is doing Facebook Live as if everybody has a TV program. It's so easy to take the little you know, get your phone, and go live on social media. And if someone comes on your broadcast from overseas, now you have an international ministry.

People like this get a little knowledge in a certain area and are ready for God to send them to the nations, promote them, and make their name and face known, but they have no virtue. They can operate in power and have all the knowledge of how to cast out devils, heal the sick, and prophesy, but their character is messed up.

Virtue has the power to make a person whole. Virtue is a life force that flows from Christ. The woman who touched Jesus in Luke 8 was made whole and was told to go in peace. The power Jesus had that healed the sick is called virtue. Jesus felt virtue leaving His body. This indicates that virtue can be measured. Multitudes were healed and made whole through the virtue that flowed from Christ. There was enough virtue in Christ to heal them all (Luke 9:11).

Virtue can produce miracles inasmuch as it can cause you

to be holy. The virtue in Christ—both in power and in character—can be accessed by faith. Faith, therefore, is a conduit through which virtue flows. You can use your faith to receive virtue from the Lord.

A VOICE WITHOUT VIRTUE

God loves virtue, but in the church today we don't emphasize it. We emphasize knowledge, reading books, going to seminars, and learning the Hebrew and Greek meanings of words, but we don't put a priority on virtue. God has shown me that if we want to walk in the power of God and see our voices and gifts truly have an effect in the earth, we must have virtue.

What God is doing now is exposing some of these ministers who have big names. They preach the house down at big conferences, but they can't live right. They have no virtue, no character. The sad part about it is that many people, including God's people, don't even care. They attend churches where the thought is, "As long as you can preach me happy and give me a good message, I don't care. What you do is your business. I'm not concerned about your lifestyle."

We've lowered the standard of what it means to be a man or woman of God. If we could raise the standard to God's standard—a righteous and virtuous standard—and stop going to their meetings and supporting their ministries, then they would have to make a choice: "Either I am going to change the way I live, or I'm not going to have a ministry." If you know they're full of bad character—they're not living clean; they're rude, mean, arrogant, controlling, and dominating—and you uphold the standard of virtue for what you allow in your own life, then they will be challenged to change.

Instead of holding ourselves and our leaders accountable, some of us have fallen back on the verse, "The gifts and
calling of God are without repentance" (Rom. 11:29), which
means we can have a gift but not live right and the gift keeps
working. We think we can keep operating in the power of the
gift while treating people badly. Somehow we feel that if our
gift is still working, God approves of unclean lifestyles, pride,
and meanness. But He doesn't.

YOU CAN LIVE RIGHT

It seems many in the body of Christ have embraced the
thinking that no one has the right to judge anybody. Some
say everyone sins every day. This thinking is used to excuse
both the body and its leaders, but it is a lie from the enemy.
You can live right. You can live virtuously. You can have
the fruit of the Spirit. You can live in love and humility. If
you are sinning every day, then you are not saved. I understand that anyone can make a mistake, but it shouldn't be
habitual. We often hear believers say, "We are sinners. We
all sin. Therefore, we can't judge anybody." But the Bible says,
"He that committeth sin is of the devil; for the devil sinneth
from the beginning. For this purpose the Son of God was
manifested, that he might destroy the works of the devil" (1
John 3:8).

Don't buy into the lie that no one can live righteously. The
whole purpose of salvation is to give us victory over sin and
reconnect us to God that, through the power of the Spirit of
God, we may be holy as He is holy. Anybody can have a bad
day. But you should not have 364 of them, when the one good
day you had, the reason you didn't sin was because you slept
all day.

No; God wants to set us free from this religious mindset that all of us are sinners. That mindset loves to put everyone in the same boat—that "everyone is a sinner" is our center and standard. They want to put everyone on the same level with them, which allows them to not even try to not curse, lie, talk about people, and lust. For some it may sound impossible to abstain from those actions, but it is possible with God to live purely and with virtue.

This is why the Lord showed me that we should add to our faith virtue, and *then* to our virtue knowledge. Virtue comes before you get into all the deep stuff. Don't be so quick to get all that knowledge that you skip over virtue.

Having knowledge without virtue means your life will be open to certain things, and you may then find yourself caught up in habitual sin and unholy behaviors. Your lifestyle will not be virtuous enough to maintain. You can have a great singing voice, write books, preach the house down, and be in a high position with all kinds of titles yet be proud, arrogant, and rude. You can go to seminary, have all the revelation, know all the Hebrew, and be ordained yet abuse and manipulate people. You can be in whatever pulpit or marketplace position opened to you, "preaching" your message your way, and have no virtue, no purity, no righteousness, and no representation of the character of God.

YOUR LIFE IS YOUR VOICE

We must understand that most of the people we meet in the marketplace or in our everyday lives will not know what we know. They will not know anything about the prophetic, speaking in tongues, the apostolic, deliverance and curses, and leviathan, Jezebel, and python spirits. You may have studied all these things and know how to cast out devils and where they dwell in different parts of the body—the back, shoulders, muscles, joints, bones, marrow, stomach, lungs, or spine. You may know how to call them by name and cast them out. Most people do not know this kind of thing. But what they do know and will be won by is your kindness, patience, and love—your humble service, purity, and reverence (1 Cor. 9:19; 1 Pet. 3:2). Jesus said they will know we are His disciples by our love (John 13:35)—not by how much we know and how much authority it appears we walk in.

How can we minister to people without virtue—compassion, kindness, humility, gentleness, patience, forgiveness, and love? Serving others without virtue is difficult. Working with people is not easy without humility, patience, forgiveness, and love. I will talk about this more in the next chapter. You cannot successfully be in relationship with people at any level for too long without virtue. But virtue is what God showed me people often forget they need when they want to be a voice, lead a ministry, or be influential in the marketplace.

We study and get all this knowledge; we get into the depths of the Word of God; we take time to read and learn the ins and outs of a Christian life. In some cases, depending on our call, we may even come to have more knowledge than some in leadership.

But you also must have enough virtue, humility, and love where God is getting ready to send you—so much that even though you may know more than most people, you never lift yourself up or look down on people who may not know what you know. Hear me when I say that you can get puffed up when you get into certain realms of the apostolic and prophetic, deliverance, the song of the Lord, worship, and the glory realm—the things of God most people on this planet are not familiar with. You will learn scriptures most people do not know. If you don't have virtue, you will get puffed up, and others' ignorance will vex you. If you don't have virtue, you'll start being mean and looking down on people, and that bitterness and pride will destroy the platform and voice God graces you with.

Proverbs 16:18 says, "Pride goeth before destruction, and an haughty spirit before a fall." We are seeing many leading voices in the body of Christ falling because they have no virtue. As a voice who represents heaven, you need the virtues of God to be the foundation on which you stand.

WHAT ARE THE VIRTUES YOUR VOICE NEEDS?

So what are these virtues? Some of them are listed as fruit of the Spirit (Gal. 5:22–23), for if we walk in the Spirit, we will bear the fruit of the Spirit. We can also find many of them in Proverbs and other places in the Bible. They are prevalent topics of discussion in timeless writings on philosophy, ethics, religion, and morality.

Over the next several pages I am going to introduce you to many of the virtues we should strive to have and cultivate in our lives even before we come to know what we are called to speak into. I will give you scriptures, definitions, quotes, and other writings about these virtues. This will help create a picture of how these virtues come together to represent Christ's life and allow His power to flow to us and through us.

Humility

Likewise, ye younger, submit yourselves unto the elder. Yea, all of you be subject one to another, and be clothed

> with humility: for God resisteth the proud, and giveth
> grace to the humble.
>
> —1 PETER 5:5

The 1828 edition of Webster's Dictionary defines humility like this: "In ethics, freedom from pride and arrogance; humbleness of mind; a modest estimate of one's own worth. In theology, *humility* consists in lowliness of mind; a deep sense of one's own unworthiness in the sight of God, self-abasement, penitence for sin, and submission to the divine will."[7]

St. Augustine is widely quoted as saying that "humility is the foundation of all the other virtues: hence, in the soul in which this virtue does not exist there cannot be any other virtue except in mere appearance."[8] Then in his book *The Heart of Virtue*, Donald DeMarco tells us that "Saint Augustine maintains that humility is the first, second, and third most important factor in religion. It is, in his judgment, the foundation of all other virtues. Consequently, there can be no virtue in the soul in which humility is lacking, only the appearance of virtue."[9]

Humility is the prerequisite to receiving the grace of God. The Bible says that "God resists the proud, but gives grace to the humble" (Jas. 4:6, NKJV). We cannot walk in virtue without the grace of God. Humility is the cornerstone of living a virtuous life.

Meekness

> With all lowliness and meekness, with longsuffering, forbearing one another in love.
>
> —EPHESIANS 4:2

"Softness of temper; mildness; gentleness; forbearance under injuries and provocations. In an evangelical sense, humility; resignation; submission to the divine will, without murmuring or peevishness; opposed to pride, arrogance and refractoriness. Galatians 5:23. I beseech you by the meekness of Christ. 1 Corinthians 10:1. Meekness is a grace which Jesus alone inculcated, and which no ancient philosopher seems to have understood or recommended."[10]

Honor

> Render therefore to all their dues: tribute to whom tribute is due; custom to whom custom; fear to whom fear; honour to whom honour.
>
> —ROMANS 13:7

Honor means "respecting those over you and acting in a way that is deserving of respect from those under you. Honor is the reputation and alliance that you earn from those you serve and those who serve you."[11]

Generosity

> The liberal soul shall be made fat: and he that watereth shall be watered also himself.
>
> —PROVERBS 11:25

Generosity is "the quality of being generous; liberality in principle; a disposition to give liberally or to bestow favors; a quality of the heart or mind opposed to meanness or parsimony."[12]

Courage

> Only be thou strong and very courageous, that thou mayest observe to do according to all the law, which Moses my servant commanded thee: turn not from it to the right hand or to the left, that thou mayest prosper withersoever thou goest.
>
> —JOSHUA 1:7

Courage is "bravery; intrepidity; that quality of mind which enables men to encounter danger and difficulties with firmness, or without fear or depression of spirits; valor; boldness; resolution. It is a constituent part of fortitude; but fortitude implies patience to bear continued suffering."[13]

I agree with what poet Maya Angelou once said: "Courage is the most important of all the virtues. Because without courage, you cannot practice any other virtue consistently."[14]

Frugality

> There is treasure to be desired and oil in the dwelling of
> the wise; but a foolish man spendeth it up.
>
> —PROVERBS 21:20

According to the 1828 edition of Webster's Dictionary, frugality is defined as "prudent economy; good husbandry or housewifery; a sparing use or appropriation of money or commodities; a judicious use of any thing to be expended or employed; that careful management of money or goods which expends nothing unnecessarily, and applies what is used to a profitable purpose; that use in which nothing is wasted. It is not equivalent to parsimony, the latter being an excess of frugality and a fault. Frugality is always a virtue. Nor is it synonymous with thrift, in its proper sense; for thrift is the effect of frugality. Without frugality none can become rich, and with it few would be poor. A prudent and sparing use or appropriation of any thing; as frugality of praise."[15]

Temperance

> It is not good to eat much honey: so for men to search
> their own glory is not glory.
>
> —PROVERBS 25:27

Temperance is "moderation; particularly, habitual moderation in regard to the indulgence of the natural appetites and passions; restrained or moderate indulgence; as temperance in eating and drinking; temperance in the indulgence of joy or mirth. Temperance in eating and drinking is opposed to gluttony and drunkenness, and in other indulgences, to excess."[16]

Kindness

> She opens her mouth with wisdom, and on her tongue is the law of kindness.
>
> —Proverbs 31:26, nkjv

Good will and *benevolence* are words that describe kindness. But the dictionary goes further to say that it is "that temper or disposition which delights in contributing to the happiness of others, which is exercised cheerfully in gratifying their wishes, supplying their wants or alleviating their distresses; benignity of nature. Kindness ever accompanies love."[17]

Patience

> Rest in the Lord, and wait patiently for him: fret not thyself because of him who prospereth in his way, because of the man who bringeth wicked devices to pass.
>
> —Psalm 37:7

Patience is characterized by "the suffering of afflictions, pain, toil, calamity, provocation or other evil, with a calm, unruffled temper; endurance without murmuring or fretfulness. Patience may spring from constitutional fortitude, from a kind of heroic pride, or from christian submission to the divine will. A calm temper which bears evils without murmuring or discontent."[18]

Fortitude

> So that we ourselves glory in you in the churches of God for your patience and faith in all your persecutions and tribulations that ye endure.
>
> —2 THESSALONIANS 1:4

Fortitude is courageous endurance—"that strength or firmness of mind or soul which enables a person to encounter danger with coolness and courage, or to bear pain or adversity without murmuring, depression or despondency," as Webster's 1828 dictionary defines it.[19] It is "the basis or source of genuine courage or intrepidity in danger, of patience in suffering, of forbearance under injuries, and of magnanimity in all conditions of life. We sometimes confound the effect with the cause, and use fortitude as synonymous with courage or patience; but courage is an active virtue or vice, and patience is the effect of fortitude. Fortitude is the guard and support of the other virtues."[20]

Steadfastness

> Therefore, my beloved brethren, be ye stedfast, unmoveable, always abounding in the work of the Lord, forasmuch as ye know that your labour is not in vain in the Lord.
>
> —1 CORINTHIANS 15:58

Steadfastness means that you exhibit a "firmness of standing; fixedness in place. Firmness of mind or purpose; fixedness in principle; constancy; resolution; as the stedfastness of faith."[21]

Tolerance

> As for the one who is weak in faith, welcome him, but not
> to quarrel over opinions. One person believes he may eat
> anything, while the weak person eats only vegetables. Let
> not the one who eats despise the one who abstains, and
> let not the one who abstains pass judgment on the one
> who eats, for God has welcomed him. Who are you to
> pass judgment on the servant of another? It is before his
> own master that he stands or falls. And he will be upheld,
> for the Lord is able to make him stand.
>
> —ROMANS 14:1–4, ESV

Tolerance is "allowing other people to have their opinions
about non-essential things and accepting the preferences and
ideas that are different from ours without compromising our
own beliefs."[22]

Prudence

> I wisdom dwell with prudence, and find out knowledge of
> witty inventions.
>
> —PROVERBS 8:12

Prudence is the virtue that allows us to determine what's
right and what's wrong and then act accordingly. Prudence
could also be called wisdom.[23]

Modesty

> In like manner also, that women adorn themselves in
> modest apparel, with shamefacedness and sobriety; not
> with broided hair, or gold, or pearls, or costly array.
>
> —1 TIMOTHY 2:9

Modesty refers to a "purity of heart in action, especially in
regards to dress and speech."[24]

Compassion

> Finally, all of you be of one mind, having compassion
> for one another; love as brothers, be tenderhearted, be
> courteous.
>
> —1 PETER 3:8, NKJV

Compassion has to do with "suffering with another" and showing "painful sympathy."[25] It is "a sensation of sorrow excited by the distress or misfortunes of another; pity; commiseration. Compassion is a mixed passion, compounded of love and sorrow; at least some portion of love generally attends the pain or regret, or is excited by it. Extreme distress of an enemy even changes enmity into at least temporary affection."[26]

Courtesy

> Finally, be ye all of one mind, having compassion one of
> another, love as brethren, be pitiful, be courteous.
>
> —1 PETER 3:8

Courtesy is "treating other people with respect, recognizing that all are made in God's image and likeness."[27]

Forgiveness

> And be ye kind one to another, tenderhearted, forgiving
> one another, even as God for Christ's sake hath forgiven
> you.
>
> —EPHESIANS 4:32

Forgiveness is "the act of forgiving; the pardon of an offender, by which he is considered and treated as not guilty. The forgiveness of enemies is a christian duty. The pardon or remission of an offense or crime; as the forgiveness of sin or of injuries."[28]

Diligence

> The hand of the diligent shall bear rule: but the slothful
> shall be under tribute.
>
> —Proverbs 12:24

"Steady application in business of any kind" is what characterizes diligence. It is the "constant effort to accomplish what is undertaken; exertion of body or mind without unnecessary delay or sloth; due attention; industry; assiduity."[29]

Gentleness

> And the servant of the Lord must not strive; but be gentle
> unto all men, apt to teach, patient.
>
> —2 Timothy 2:24
>
> Throw away thy rod, throw away thy wrath: O my God,
> take the gentle path.[30]
>
> —George Herbert

Gentleness is defined as "softness of manners; mildness of temper; sweetness of disposition; meekness."[31]

Equity

> Then shalt thou understand righteousness, and judgment,
> and equity; yea, every good path.
>
> —Proverbs 2:9

Webster's 1828 dictionary says that "in practice, equity is the impartial distribution of justice, or the doing that to another which the laws of God and man, and of reason, give him a right to claim. It is the treating of a person according to justice and reason."[32]

Truth

> Let not mercy and truth forsake thee: bind them about
> thy neck; write them upon the table of thine heart.
> —PROVERBS 3:3

Truth is "veracity; purity from falsehood; practice of speaking truth; habitual disposition to speak truth; as when we say, a man is a man of truth."[33]

Mercy

> Blessed are the merciful: for they shall obtain mercy.
> —MATTHEW 5:7

Mercy is "that benevolence, mildness or tenderness of heart which disposes a person to overlook injuries, or to treat an offender better than he deserves." It is "the disposition that tempers justice, and induces an injured person to forgive trespasses and injuries, and to forbear punishment, or inflict less than law or justice will warrant."[34]

Webster's goes on to say, "There is perhaps no word in our language precisely synonymous with mercy. That which comes nearest to it is grace. It implies benevolence, tenderness, mildness, pity or compassion, and clemency, but exercised only towards offenders. Mercy is a distinguishing attribute of the Supreme Being."[35]

Peaceableness

> But the wisdom that is from above is first pure, then
> peaceable, gentle, and easy to be intreated, full of mercy
> and good fruits, without partiality, and without hypocrisy.
> —JAMES 3:17

Peaceableness, according to Webster's 1828 dictionary, is "the state of being peaceable; quietness." It is a "disposition to peace."[36]

Godliness

> For bodily exercise profiteth little: but godliness is profitable unto all things, having promise of the life that now is, and of that which is to come.
>
> —1 Timothy 4:8

Godliness is defined as "piety; belief in God, and reverence for his character and laws. A religious life; a careful observance of the laws of God and performance of religious duties, proceeding from love and reverence for the divine character and commands; christian obedience."[37]

Cleanliness

> The fear of the Lord is clean, enduring for ever: the judgments of the Lord are true and righteous altogether.
>
> —Psalm 19:9

Webster's 1828 dictionary gives us two definitions for *cleanliness*: "freedom from dirt, filth, or any foul, extraneous matter" and "neatness of person or dress; purity."[38]

Orderliness

> Let all things be done decently and in order.
>
> —1 Corinthians 14:40

Orderliness is "regularity; a state of being methodical. The state of being orderly."[39]

Loyalty

A friend loveth at all times, and a brother is born for adversity.

—PROVERBS 17:17

According to [American philosopher Josiah] Royce, loyalty is a virtue, indeed a primary virtue, "the heart of all the virtues, the central duty amongst all the duties.".…The short definition that he gives of the idea is that loyalty is "the willing and practical and thoroughgoing devotion of a person to a cause."[40]

Collins English Dictionary defines loyalty as "the quality of staying firm in your friendship or support for someone or something."[41]

Faithfulness

A faithful man shall abound with blessings: but he that maketh haste to be rich shall not be innocent.

—PROVERBS 28:20

Faithfulness is synonymous with "fidelity," "loyalty," "truth," and "veracity."[42] It is the "firm adherence to allegiance and duty; as the faithfulness of a subject" or "the faithfulness of God."[43] It is also characterized by "strict adherence to injunctions, and to the duties of a station; as the faithfulness of servants or ministers. Strict performance of promises, vows or covenants; constancy in affection; as the faithfulness of a husband or wife."[44]

The writers at AgapeLife.org say that "faithfulness is a core trait we see the importance of over and over in scripture. There is a big connection to faith in God and faithfulness (Luke 6:46). God seeks the faithful and loyal of heart."[45]

Charity

> And above all these things put on charity, which is the
> bond of perfectness.
>
> —COLOSSIANS 3:14

Then in the Amplified Bible the same passage reads:
"Beyond all these things put on and wrap yourselves in
[unselfish] love, which is the perfect bond of unity [for everything is bound together in agreement when each one seeks
the best for others]."

Generally charity is connected to "love, benevolence, good
will; that disposition of heart which inclines men to think
favorably of their fellow man, and to do them good. In a
theological sense, it includes supreme love to God, and uni-
versal good will to men. 1 Corinthians 8:1. Colossians 3:14.
1 Timothy 1:5."[46] More specifically it is connected to "love,
kindness, affection, tenderness, springing from natural rela-
tions; as the charities of father, son and brother."[47]

Other ways charity is seen is in "liberality to the poor, consisting in almsgiving or benefactions, or in gratuitous services to relieve them in distress. Alms; whatever is bestowed
gratuitously on the poor for their relief."[48] We also tend to
think of it in terms of "liberality in gifts and services to promote public objects of utility, as to found and support bible
societies, missionary societies, and others."[49]

Reverence

> Wherefore we receiving a kingdom which cannot be
> moved, let us have grace, whereby we may serve God
> acceptably with reverence and godly fear.
>
> —HEBREWS 12:28

Reverence is "fear mingled with respect and esteem; veneration."[50]

"When quarrels and factions are carried openly," Webster's 1828 dictionary explains, "it is a sign that the reverence of government is lost. The fear acceptable to God, is a filial fear, an awful reverence of the divine nature, proceeding from a just esteem of his perfections, which produces in us an inclination to his service and an unwillingness to offend him."[51]

Honesty

> Let us walk honestly, as in the day; not in rioting and drunkenness, not in chambering and wantonness, not in strife and envying.
>
> —ROMANS 13:13

"In principle," honesty is "an upright disposition; moral rectitude of heart; a disposition to conform to justice and correct moral principles, in all social transactions. In fact, upright conduct; an actual conformity to justice and moral rectitude. Fairness; candor; truth; as the honesty of a narrative. Frank sincerity. Honesty is chiefly applicable to social transactions, or mutual dealings in the exchange of property."[52]

Chastity

> For I am jealous over you with godly jealousy: for I have espoused you to one husband, that I may present you as a chaste virgin to Christ.
>
> —2 CORINTHIANS 11:2

> Chastity is the most unpopular of the Christian virtues.[53]
>
> —C. S. LEWIS

Chasity is "purity of the body; freedom from all unlawful commerce of sexes."[54] Chastity before marriage is "purity from all commerce of sexes," and after marriage, it ought to continue as "fidelity [or faithfulness] to the marriage bed."[55] When you have the virtue of chastity, you live in a place of "freedom from obscenity, as in language or conversation; freedom from bad mixture; purity in words and phrases."[56] It is also defined as "purity; unadulterated state; as the chastity of the gospel."[57]

Hope

> Who against hope believed in hope, that he might become
> the father of many nations, according to that which was
> spoken, so shall thy seed be.
>
> —ROMANS 4:18

Hope is "desire of some good, accompanied with at least a slight expectation of obtaining it, or a belief that it is obtainable. Hope differs from wish and desire in this, that it implies some expectation of obtaining the good desired, or the possibility of possessing it. Hope therefore always gives pleasure or joy; whereas wish and desire may produce or be accompanied with pain and anxiety."[58]

Hope is also defined as a sense of "confidence in a future event; the highest degree of well founded expectation of good; as a hope founded on God's gracious promises; a scriptural sense."[59]

It can also be seen in "that which gives hope; he or that which furnishes ground of expectation, or promises desired good. The hope of Israel is the Messiah."[60]

Faith

> For therein is the righteousness of God revealed from
> faith to faith: as it is written, The just shall live by faith.
>
> —ROMANS 1:17

Faith is "belief" or "the assent of the mind to the truth of what is declared by another, resting on his authority and veracity, without other evidence; the judgment that what another states or testifies is the truth." For example, "I have strong faith or no faith in the testimony of a witness, or in what a historian narrates."[61]

Integrity

> The integrity of the upright shall guide them: but the perverseness of transgressors shall destroy them.
>
> —Proverbs 11:3

It has been said that "nothing more completely baffles one who is full of tricks and duplicity than straightforward and simple integrity in another."[62] Integrity has to do with "the entire, unimpaired state of any thing, particularly of the mind; moral soundness or purity; incorruptness; uprightness; honesty. Integrity comprehends the whole moral character, but has a special reference to uprightness in mutual dealings, transfers of property, and agencies for others."[63]

As Kerby Anderson, radio-show host and president of Probe Ministries International, wrote:

> The word *integrity* comes from the same Latin root as *integer* and implies a wholeness of person. Just as we would talk about a whole number, so also we can talk about a whole person who is undivided. A person of integrity is living rightly, not divided, nor being a different person in different circumstances. A person of integrity is the same person in private that he or she is in public.[64]

Gratitude

> And let the peace of God rule in your hearts, to the which
> also ye are called in one body; and be ye thankful.
>
> —COLOSSIANS 3:15

Gratitude is defined as "an emotion of the heart, excited by a favor or benefit received; a sentiment of kindness or good will towards a benefactor; thankfulness. Gratitude is an agreeable emotion, consisting in or accompanied with good will to a benefactor, and a disposition to make a suitable return of benefits or services, or when no return can be made, with a desire to see the benefactor prosperous and happy. Gratitude is a virtue of the highest excellence, as it implies a feeling and generous heart, and a proper sense of duty."[65]

Sincerity

> Grace be with all them that love our Lord Jesus Christ in
> sincerity. Amen.
>
> —EPHESIANS 6:24

Sincerity is "honesty of mind or intention; freedom from simulation or hypocrisy. We may question a man's prudence, when we cannot question his sincerity. Freedom from hypocrisy, disguise or false pretense; as the sincerity of a declaration or of love."[66]

Joy

> Then he said unto them, Go your way, eat the fat, and
> drink the sweet, and send portions unto them for whom
> nothing is prepared: for this day is holy unto our LORD:
> neither be ye sorry; for the joy of the LORD is your
> strength.
>
> —NEHEMIAH 8:10

Joy is another fruit of the Spirit. I believe joy is one of the most important virtues because it releases strength. We are to serve God with joy. Joy is one-third of the kingdom (Rom. 14:17). Joy comes from within and is not contingent upon the circumstances around us.

Goodness

> But the fruit of the Spirit is love, joy, peace, longsuffering, gentleness, goodness, faith.
> —GALATIANS 5:22

> Virtue is the power to do good.[67]
> —MIKE HICKEY

Goodness is "the state of being good; the physical qualities which constitute value, excellence or perfection; as the goodness of timber; the goodness of a soil."[68] It includes "the moral qualities which constitute christian excellence; moral virtue; religion. The fruit of the Spirit is love, joy, peace, long-suffering, gentleness, goodness, faith. Galatians 5:22. Kindness; benevolence; benignity of heart; but more generally, acts of kindness; charity; humanity exercised. I shall remember his goodness to me with gratitude."[69]

Hospitality

> A bishop then must be blameless, the husband of one wife, vigilant, sober, of good behaviour, given to hospitality, apt to teach.
> —1 TIMOTHY 3:2

Hospitality is "the act or practice of receiving and entertaining strangers or guests without reward, or with kind and generous liberality."[70]

Merriam-Webster defines *hospitable* in these terms:

- given to generous and cordial reception of guests

- offering a pleasant and sustaining environment

- readily receptive: open

- ready or willing to accept or consider something[71]

Realize that being hospitable is not only linked to how you welcome people in your home. It is also related to how you receive and treat others. What is your personal disposition? Are you inviting and welcoming as a person? Are you open to considering new ideas and receiving new people?

We may be inclined to think of hospitality in terms of how clean our house is when guests arrive or how well we feed them. However, the full meaning of this virtue challenges each of us to evaluate how we are as a person.

VIRTUE IS A NECESSITY FOR EVERY VOICE

As you read through the list of virtues, you may have realized that you are stronger in some areas than others. But I want you to work with those areas in which you're not strong. If it's humility, meekness, being teachable, being corrected, being accountable, being patient, or being kind, commit to increasing in those virtues. Even as I mention kindness, again I am reminded of how much this virtue is needed in the church. We need to know how to talk to people, how to be kind to people. Some people say, "I'm prophetic. I just tell it like it is." No, they are just mean and bitter. You can rebuke and correct people and still be kind. You can walk in kindness and humility.

Wherever you are lacking, you can be strengthened. God can bring up the difference and bring proper balance into your life. Understand that these virtues are not dictated by personality type. They are about you carrying the right sound to activate the heavens and bring others into the kingdom. This is about you showing the handiwork and glory of God. This is about you having the right heart and mind as you take territory and overthrow darkness. You now understand that what may seem impossible about developing good character and moral excellence in that way is possible with God.

Yes, you may have to reach out to God and put a demand on Him to release His virtue in your life. We can often get into a place where we just want God to touch us, change us, heal us, or restore us. But Jesus said, "You don't have to wait for Me to touch you. You can touch Me." The woman in the Bible with the issue of blood didn't wait for Jesus to come and lay hands on her. (See Luke 8:43–48.) She pressed through the crowd, touched the hem of His garment, and received her miracle.

Listen, you have a call on your life that you have been pressing toward and pursuing. You may have attended every conference and read every book. You may have received one prophetic word after another. You may be surrounded by a bunch of people who don't know what you know about who God has called you to be. But you'd better press through everything, because as you press through and touch Jesus, His virtue will come into your life.

And as it did for the woman with the issue of blood, Jesus'

virtue flowing in your life will remove every issue. You will not continue to have the issues you've had in the past. I prophesy that as you seek to expand the kingdom of God by amplifying your voice, poverty will not be your issue; lack will not be your issue; sickness will not be your issue; hurt, bitterness, and pride will not be your issues. Loneliness will not be your issue. Declare it now: "These things will not be my issues as the virtue of Jesus comes into my life." Declare that every issue in your life is being stopped now. They are drying up by the virtue of God.

Virtue brings wholeness and excellence to your life. Virtue is the atmosphere of power, healing, and miracles. The virtuous life is the admired and respected life. Jesus was a man of virtue. He is our perfect example of the power of virtue. We can walk in this virtue by living a Christlike life. His life can affect every part of our being and cause us to live in the realm of power and glory.

If you believe this and want to have the virtue of Christ in your life, pray this prayer with me now.

PRAYER FOR AN IMPARTATION OF CHRISTLIKE VIRTUE

Father, I ask that You will impart a greater measure of kindness, grace, humility, meekness, long-suffering, and gentleness into my life. I pray that as I walk in virtue, I will experience the chayil *of God. Let virtue increase that even when I minister, people will be healed and delivered because Your virtue is being released out of me.*

I pray today as I reach up and touch You, Jesus, that Your virtue flows into me. Lord, I receive my virtue. I touch You today. Thank You for allowing Your virtue to come into my life. Amen.

CHAPTER 7

THE VOICE THAT SUFFERS LONG

Therefore, as the elect of God, holy and
beloved, put on tender mercies, kindness,
humility, meekness, longsuffering.

—COLOSSIANS 3:12, NKJV

I N THE LAST chapter I discussed a list of virtues that you need as a representative of heaven, as one who speaks and heaven responds. You must understand that with a great calling comes a great responsibility to operate in integrity, prudence, wisdom, humility, kindness, and love. These are traits that show you have been sent by God. I've taught many lessons on wisdom, as it is the principal thing, as Proverbs 4:7 says. It unlocks the favor of God.

I could teach all day on wisdom and favor. However, there is another virtue I want to spend some time on. It is not one we like to bring up too often, but I consider this virtue critical when it comes to being able to speak into people's lives, political or social issues, trends and innovations in the marketplace, and things that advance the kingdom. That virtue is long-suffering.

Long-suffering is defined as "patiently enduring lasting offense or hardship." Synonyms include "Forbearing," "patient," "tolerant," and "uncomplaining." "Suffering for a long time without complaining: very patient during difficult times" is another dimension of long-suffering.[1] It is a fruit of the Spirit found in Galatians 5:22–23. It is part of Paul's urgent request to the Ephesian church and even for us today. He urges that we walk worthy of our call "with longsuffering, forbearing one another in love" (Eph. 4:2).

I can imagine what you're thinking. This doesn't sound like a feel-good, preach-me-happy kind of message. This sounds hard. And we really didn't need to look up the definition of long-suffering to know it is not something our flesh naturally wants to do.

Who do you know that carries this virtue? Just looking at the word, you can see that it is made up of two words we don't like when they're put together: *suffering* and *long*. We can deal with short suffering, but when's the last time you heard a message on long-suffering? The church doesn't often address that, but I want to discuss it in terms of being a voice in the earth, speaking into situations, and bringing heaven to earth. We need long-suffering in order to bring heaven into people's hells on earth. People are in situations where their sin or ignorance—or the sins or ignorance of their fathers and mothers, grandfathers and grandmothers—have gotten them into some messed-up situations. And you may be the one voice in their lives that changes everything.

Long-suffering is also a key to standing firm through persecution. This comes in many forms, but at the time of Paul's letters to the Galatians and Ephesians, the church was facing persecution in the form of physical imprisonment, torture, and death. The believers had been under fire since the days of Acts, after the Holy Spirit came into the Upper Room like a mighty, rushing wind and many were added to the church in Jerusalem. They came under heavy persecution during that time and had to flee the city. But as they scattered, the gospel spread like fire. God used the persecution as a way to push the early church out of its comfort zone. It was as if He said, "If you're not going to leave this area and preach the gospel, I'm going to make you go out."

Even today the global church is facing persecution in countries like China and in parts of the Middle East. According to a statement from Anglican Bishop Philip Mounstephen published by the BBC, "Evidence shows not only the geographic spread of anti-Christian persecution, but also its increasing severity....In some regions, the level and nature of persecution is arguably coming close to meeting the international definition of genocide."[2] Reports also indicate an exponential spread of the gospel in those areas. The kingdom expands at greater levels when there is persecution, because persecution brings forth the voice of heaven. God puts a demand on the prophetic voice when His kingdom suffers violence.

Persecution can come in many ways. Have you felt you've had a target on your back since even before you were born? I've heard many testimonies and ministered to many believers whose destinies were threatened by abortion, rejection, abandonment, shame, and abuse. So many things may have tried to silence you before you learned the power of your voice. And even as you've come into the knowledge of who God has called you to be, you are coming against all kinds of opposition that is trying to silence you. Unusual bouts with laryngitis, attacks in your sleep, tightness in your throat, imposter syndrome, attacks against your confidence, and writer's block are common things that come against preachers, speakers, writers, songwriters, minstrels, and worship leaders. You also may notice attacks against your finances even when you are giving. These can all be forms of spiritual persecution that come to limit your ability to move into the things to which God has called you.

The more you come into the knowledge of who God has called you to be, the more the enemy raises the level of persecution against your call. When you are facing certain trials, you should be encouraged to know that you are a threat to the kingdom of darkness.

Long-suffering means that you will be able to endure difficulties until God breaks through. Most often viewed through the lens of spiritual persecution, *long-suffering* also means you are able to endure the vexing relationships or difficult situations God is calling you to speak into. *Long-suffering* means you may need to work with some people or work through some situations until healing or deliverance comes, or until a problem is solved. You may need to keep pressing until those you are praying, decreeing, and declaring over are set free, walking upright, and prospering and in good health.

There are some circumstances in which God is calling us to suffer long, forbearing in love. There are some people with whom God is calling us to suffer long. We can't be in it for the short-term, ready to jump ship when something gets on our nerves or the situation gets too uncomfortable. As you speak into situations and understand that you are the heavens

God is speaking about in Psalm 19, you will begin to realize that you must speak until you see heaven come to earth and bring transformation in whatever situation in which God has placed you.

WHY YOU NEED LONG-SUFFERING

Long-suffering is a major virtue, and we need to add it to our faith *before* we add knowledge. Here's why: Not everyone you are called to will have it all together. Many of them will be in bad situations. They will not have the knowledge you have. But as you demonstrate long-suffering, humility, kindness, self-control, generosity, and the other virtues, you will see their situations turn around. Without long-suffering, you will be vexed by their ignorance.

The Bible says in Ecclesiastes 1:18, "For in much wisdom is much grief: and he that increaseth knowledge increaseth sorrow." The more you know, the more sorrowful you can become. You can look around at all the ignorance and what people do with their lives, and it can make you cry. Sometimes when people come to me for a prophetic word or prayer and the Lord reveals to me what they are dealing with, I want to just weep. Because they don't know how to live, they are making choices that are literally messing up their lives.

When God has brought you out of the life you were in, it can be hard to watch others struggle in theirs. But many times they won't study, pray, and learn how to grow in God. They don't want to pay the price to live for God and be blessed. Then they look at you and others who are studying and learning and adding to your faith virtue and to virtue knowledge, and get jealous.

You were in every service. You were at the altar, crying

out to God. You were fasting, praying, and confessing the Word. You did what it took to break through, and the others didn't. You went to conferences and spent all your money on resources and books. Then you went home and studied for days and weeks while they were doing other stuff. You obtained knowledge and wisdom. You were building your faith. You learned what it meant to move in the prophetic and apostolic; in deliverance, healing, and miracles; in worship and glory while they were doing what they wanted to do. But then when they get in trouble, they want to come to you for prayer. Can you relate to this? *They* didn't want to take the time to study and pray, but then *they* want to run to you to get you to pray for them. They had time for sin but not to grow spiritually.

Do you see how easily you can become vexed—angered, frustrated, annoyed, and irritated—if you obtain all the knowledge but have no virtue, no long-suffering? "If they just knew about deliverance," you shake your head and think, "they wouldn't be dealing with stuff they could have been freed from."

We love knowledge. We love it more than we love virtue, because virtue is to walk in humility. Virtue is to have long-suffering and patience. Virtue is to be filled with love, charity, godliness, honesty, integrity, goodness, and mercy. Virtue is to show compassion. These are the things God says we need to develop in our lives even before we obtain knowledge. He always knows best. He sees the end from the beginning. He wants you to add to your faith virtue so that by the time you have knowledge, you can also have compassion. Then you can have compassion on people who don't know what you know about the goodness, grace, and love of God.

I remember one day I was downtown in Chicago, and as I was coming out of a store, a young man and his son walked up to me, and the young man said, "Sir, do you have any change?"

I said, "What are you doing out here asking for change? This is not God's plan for your life. What church do you go to?"

He said, "I go to church."

I said, "What church?"

"I go to Saint Peter's around the corner."

I said, "You need to go to Saint Peter's and get a refund. Because they're not teaching you anything, brother. You are begging on the street. This is not the will of God. Let me pray for you." (When people ask you for money, they will let you pray for them because they know money's coming.)

I began to pray for him right there on the street as several people walked by, and he began to weep like a baby. The tears fell so hard they were running down his face and dropping to the ground. The man wasn't used to somebody wanting to pray for him. He may have expected me to just pull some money and keep moving. He wasn't expecting me to take time with him and get to the root of why he was standing on the street begging with his young son.

I began to pray: "God, I break every spirit of poverty and lack that is causing this man to be out here with his son begging on the streets. I break every spirit of shame and come against any spirits that are hindering him." Then I prophesied over him.

Tears continued to gush out of his eyes.

Sometimes people just need compassion. It's already bad enough that he was at a place in his life where he felt he had to beg. No one wants to be out on the street asking for money with their child. He was already stuck in shame and poverty. He did not need me to be judgmental and critical.

One thing I did do, however, was give him a loving word of rebuke. I told him, "Brother, you need to get into a house where you can learn the Word of God. I don't know what Saint Peter's is teaching you, whether it's Hail Marys or whatever. But you need a church that will help build you and your son up so you don't have to beg on the street anymore. This is not the life God had in mind for you."

We often don't know how blessed we are to know what we know about the prophetic and apostolic; deliverance and miracles; faith and healing; giving, prosperity, and abundance; worship and the song of the Lord. There aren't many people in the world who really understand these particular things. God has been good to you by bringing you into the knowledge of the truth.

STAY UNTIL THE ENEMY GOES

When we are on assignment to use our voice, gifts, talents, and even the knowledge we've gained to minister to people, we need a lot of compassion, love, and patience. We need long-suffering. You can get all this knowledge, but if you're not patient with people, you can't minister deliverance to them. Or if you are in the marketplace, you won't be a successful coach or mentor. Some people will not get delivered or launched in one session. They will keep coming back, sometimes within the same day.

In one deliverance session, I had commanded the spirit of fear to leave a person, and the demon came out. But then another spirit of fear came up. I said, "Well, I thought I cast you out."

It said, "I'm a different spirit of fear."

Another time, we were casting out demons, and I said, "Spirit of anger, come out of her." And the demon wouldn't move.

I said, "I told you to go."

It said, "My name is not anger. My name is wrath. You got the wrong demon."

I said, "Well, whatever your name is, get out of her."

Your voice can have a great impact when you have patience, compassion, mercy, and grace with people. You need virtue to be able to stick with people until they experience full and complete freedom. I thank God for the power, wealth, riches, force, and might that are characteristic of *chayil*. But we must also embrace goodness, humility, kindness, long-suffering, generosity, and gentleness. If you give yourself to this aspect of virtue, you will begin to increase the power of God in your life.

I heard prophetic minister Ryan LeStrange quote a statement from author Bill Vincent one time when he was preaching that just stuck with me. He said, "When you discover things that seem to contribute to the glory, do those things more and when you find things that seem to diminish the glory, stop doing them. It's as simple as that."[3]

INCREASING AND RESTORING VIRTUE TO YOUR VOICE

Humility, patience, long-suffering, compassion—these are godly virtues you can grow in. You should have more virtue now than you had five years ago. You should not be going to church and getting worse than you were five years ago. I've seen this happen. People go to every service. They experience the glory of God. They worship and receive deliverance ministry. But they get worse. The church is designed to make you better, not worse.

If you are a pastor, entrepreneur, or leader of an organization, you need to be long-suffering, because if you aren't, you'll get bitter. People will leave you and not even say goodbye. People you've invested in and taught everything they know will walk away from you and not even say thank you. They are like the ungrateful lepers whom Jesus healed in Luke 17:11–19 who didn't return to say thank you. Some will walk away from you and talk about you as if you're the biggest devil in town. You prayed for them, prophesied over them, laid hands on them, imparted into them, lent them your platform, and promoted them and their ministries, and they'll walk away from you and not even say goodbye.

If you don't have long-suffering, you'll end up bitter, messed up, and sick in your body. You'll be a deliverance worker who needs deliverance. You need the virtue of long-suffering in your life. When you have long-suffering, you can endure the mistreatment that will come because of the anointing of God you carry. Jesus warned us of this in the Book of John:

> If the world hates you, you know that it hated Me before it hated you. If you were of the world, the world would love you as its own. But because you are not of the world, since I chose you out of the world, the world therefore hates you. Remember the word that I said to you: "A servant is not greater than his master." If they persecuted Me, they will also persecute you. If they kept My words, they will keep yours also. But all these things they will

do to you for My name's sake, because they do not know
Him who sent Me.

—JOHN 15:18–21, MEV

He also said to shake the dust off your feet if your words
or ministry are not received (Matt. 10:14). In other words,
don't let the rejection stick to you. Don't let bitterness set in.
Forgive them and move on. Release them.

This can be hard, especially when you start out excited and
full of joy about what God has called you to. Then ten years
in, because so much has happened to you at the hands of
other people, you become jaded and angry.

I remember when I got ordained in 1981. I was twenty-four
years old at the time. The bishop called me and four other
candidates up to get our ordination papers. There was no
prophetic ministry. He didn't say, "Prophets, come and lay
hands and prophesy over these men."

All he said was, "Make sure you pay your dues every year."
Then he looked at us as if he felt sorry for us and said, "Are
you sure you want to do this?"

It was like he knew: "Oh, you all are young and excited.
You're planning to take the world for Jesus. You all are fresh—
fresh meat. The saints are about to eat you up."

I was standing there thinking, "Thank God. I'm being
ordained."

But the bishop was there like, "Are you sure you're ready
for this?"

At another time, I was participating in an ordination in
Detroit. A woman of God had asked me to come and help
her ordain some leaders. I will never forget it. It was the most
unusual ordination I have ever been a part of. The ordination rites were written out in a book, and we had to read

the candidates their charge. I couldn't believe it, but it actually said, "Now turn around and look at the congregation, for some of them will betray you and walk away from you."

I was thinking, "Man, this is a depressing ordination. Is it that bad?"

Years ago I was at a meeting where it became obvious the presiding leader of the group was getting older and was about to step down. I learned that in this case, when a leader dies, he is replaced by one of the leaders who are ranked just below him. This creates an atmosphere where everybody is waiting to become the next in line. So at this meeting the leader got up and began to read from Acts 20:29, where Paul said, "For I know this, that after my departing shall grievous wolves enter in among you, not sparing the flock." And he turned around and said, "And here they are."

Of course they may have tried to cover for him and say, "Oh, he's just getting old. He's losing his mind. Don't pay him any attention." But there they were—the next in line sitting right there waiting for him to die so they could take his place.

I don't talk about my own pastor very much, but he was a prophet of God and was saved in 1929.

Because he was a prophet, the church he was part of really didn't understand him and gave him a hard time. He would have visions, and he would draw what he saw. One time he had a vision of a meeting table, and around it were a bunch of bears. So he drew a picture of bears sitting around a table and took it to his pastors. When he told me this, I said, "No wonder they didn't like you. You brought them a picture of a bunch of bears, and they were the bears."

He would tell us all the stuff he went through in the church as a young preacher. I remember one time when we were driving from Chicago to Memphis for a conference. One of the men traveling with us and my pastor were talking about some of the stuff that goes on in the church. The other man said, "Don't say this around the young preachers. They don't need to know this."

Then my pastor said, "I am going to tell them everything I know so they can be prepared for the stuff they have to deal with."

It was good to be brought up in ministry under my pastor. He helped us know that there are people in ministry who have no virtue. They preach, they teach, and they conduct services, but they have no virtue, humility, long-suffering, patience, compassion, goodness, or mercy. They are selfish, and many times they want you to sit under them. They can prophesy, minister a word of knowledge, and operate in the gifts of the Spirit. Some can prophesy so accurately that they can call your name, your address, and your social security number, but they can't keep away from adultery and fornication. They lack self-control and holiness.

As a voice that represents the kingdom of God and speaks on behalf of heaven, you must have virtue. You must keep yourself clean and live holy. Don't use profanity. Keep your hands to yourself.

So if you want to move in the *chayil* power of God, commit to having virtue. It is not one of those things that is often celebrated, but it is of high value to God. Virtue is what you demonstrate when you're not in the pulpit or leading out front in some capacity. Virtue is what you have when you are behind closed doors.

Let me tell you one more story. You know, as you get older, you start telling stories. Years ago my wife and I were out eating at an old country buffet. I was upset about something and was arguing with her right there at the table when someone walked up and said, "Apostle Eckhardt!"

Without missing a beat, I said, "Praise the Lord!"

I shifted that quickly. I felt like such a hypocrite. Knowing how people are with each other, I knew my wife had every right to say, "Uh-huh, look at you. You have the nerve to talk about 'Praise the Lord,' when you were just chewing me out. You are supposed to be a man of God."

Whether she said these exact words or not, I felt conviction and had to start laughing. I asked her, "Would you forgive me, baby? God let somebody catch me right in public. I am so sorry."

I prophesy that, with all you carry and represent, if you act like a fool, somebody will walk up to you and say, "I really enjoy your ministry," in the middle of your meltdown. May you always hold on to virtue. And let me tell you this: when virtue hits your life, the power of God will affect every area. You will think virtuously and speak virtuously. As I've said, virtue is something we don't speak of very much now, but God is highlighting its importance, and one of the virtues you will need to develop is long-suffering. You will need this virtue so you will be able to keep calm in the midst of trials and tests and dealing with flaky people. Long-suffering, patience, and perseverance all point to the ability to withstand trials and tests without becoming bitter or angry. With these virtues you can go through hell and still keep your love. You can go through mess and still walk in integrity. You can go through betrayal and still love people.

DECLARATIONS FOR AN IMPARTATION AND INCREASE OF VIRTUE

Lord, with all diligence I will add to my faith virtue and to virtue knowledge. I will not skip virtue.

_____

Lord, I will make virtue a priority in my life.

_____

Long-suffering, gentleness, patience, meekness, humility, integrity, honesty, goodness, mercy, compassion, joy—let these virtues increase in my life.

_____

*Lord, I thank You that I am a virtuous believer. I am a **chayil** believer. And Lord, I pray that as virtue increases in my life, Your power will also increase in my life.*

_____

As humility increases in my life, Your virtue and Your power will also increase in my life.

_____

Lord, let me think virtuously. Let me speak virtuously. Let me walk virtuously. Let me minister virtuously.

_____

Thank You, Lord, that Your virtue is increasing in my life. Your power, goodness, and excellence are increasing in my life.

*I will walk in **chayil** power all the days of my life, because I have virtue.*

Thank You, Lord, for virtue and glory increasing in my life.

Lord, I commit to a virtuous lifestyle. I will live clean. I will live holy. I will walk in integrity. I will keep myself pure in every area of my life. I will handle money with purity and honesty. I will not cheat. I will not lie. I will not be dishonest.

Thank You, Lord! I will walk in virtue all the days of my life.

Father, thank You for releasing long-suffering into my life.

CHAPTER 8

CONFESS WITH YOUR MOUTH— ACTIVATING THE POWER OF THE TONGUE

Therefore whoever confesses Me before
men, him I will also confess before
My Father who is in heaven.
—MATTHEW 10:32, NKJV,
EMPHASIS ADDED

TO BE A voice that heaven responds to, you need a certain kind of atmosphere to grow, develop, and be stirred, because when you're in that kind of atmosphere, your gifts, anointing, talents, and abilities come forward. Now, there are different things that contribute to this kind of atmosphere, and really, the local church should be the place where this atmosphere is cultivated for you to be developed and to grow.

In other words, you should not be attending a not-for-*prophet* church. Though this book is not specifically about the prophetic, anyone who has been called to speak as heaven speaks or to speak in a way that heaven responds to must have a prophetic nature. As we have already seen, to speak into situations and bring heaven instead of hell, and healing and peace instead of strife and confusion, to bring the virtue and power of God, you must be prophetic. To continue to be built up and stirred in a way that allows you to grow in your ability to be a voice, you must be able to hear from God. This is the core of the prophetic realm. Local churches that accept and promote the prophetic gift and office are the most effective in helping you keep your voice sharp, accurate, and effective.

You will not flow in your calling or accomplish your assignments if you are in a church where people fight, shut down, and don't encourage or believe in the prophetic. You will end up dying in that place. You will feel stifled and eventually feel silenced. Having visions and dreams is good, but more than that, to stir your voice and see it impact the nations, you must have a desire for the glory of God.

A voice that brings heaven to earth should want to see God glorified. You should want to see God honored, served, worshipped, and prioritized. Bringing heaven to earth—seeing heaven come into people's lives; seeing heaven come in and change your family and reverse generational curses; seeing heaven come into your church, your city, or your nation—is all about God manifesting His glory, His presence, and the rule of the heavenly realm on earth. Declaring the glory of God must be your number one priority as you accomplish the thing God has set you on the earth to do. When you put anything before God, it will disturb the effectiveness of your voice. Expressing the glory of God must be your main concern. And if you are in a church that does not cultivate an environment where the glory of God dwells, it may be time to find a new one.

When giving God glory is not the number one thing, we begin to give glory to false gods, just as Israel did. We open the door to idol worship when God is not number one. Our churches and our lives become centers for serving idols and worshipping false gods. We begin breaking covenant and disobeying the voice of God, and the blessing of God is no longer evident. In that environment we compromise our influence in the heavens and in the earth. Many in the church are wondering how we lost the ability to speak into certain areas and see God's power manifest. It is because the glory of God is not the number one priority. We shut it out. If we want to be blessed and see our words carry weight in the earth, we must repent and return to a place in our hearts where God is our number one priority. We must give Him glory.

Worship is at the forefront of developing a heart that makes God the priority, because as you glorify God, you become a worshipper. There's no way you can tell me that you glorify God in your life but don't like to worship. God's glory is His presence, and He is present in praise and worship (Ps. 22:3). If God is a priority in your life, worship must be important to you. If God is the priority in your life, you must love His presence. If God is a priority in your life, when His presence is in a service, you will not be standing there with your hands in your pockets chewing gum. You will either be bowing down, lifting your hands, dancing, or weeping. True worship should always be the focus in everything you do— your priority should be what exalts God, what brings glory to His name, and what amplifies His nature.

Anytime Israel did not worship God properly, the prophets would come and rebuke them. It was always the will of God for worship not to be relegated to Jerusalem and Israel; it was always meant to go throughout the world so there would be people from every color, tribe, tongue, and language who would worship God, because our God is great. There is no one like Him in heaven or earth. He is awesome. He is magnificent. He is the greatest. He is beautiful. He is majestic. He is powerful. He is the only true and living God. When you really get a revelation of the God for whom you've been called to speak, you'll become a worshipper.

PATTERN FOR WORSHIP

In the Bible, the pattern worshipper is David, and probably more than any other person in Scripture he is the one who helps us understand the importance of worship. He loved worshipping God. He loved being in the presence of God. He was a voice that spoke on behalf of heaven and carried a prophetic mantle. There's something about being a voice and being prophetic. You can't be a voice without being prophetic. This prophetic nature requires you to have a certain kind of atmosphere of worship in order to thrive. Sometimes in our churches we've had more entertainment than we've had true worship. We love to sing. We love the music. We have great singers. We have great performers. We have gospel artists, but the problem sometimes—in America at least—is that some of the key Christian artists do not have lifestyles that are conducive to holiness.

When something only makes people clap and feel good and there is no conviction, anointing, presence, or glory, it has no real effect on our lives. So what God did through David was to establish a pattern for true worship that ushers in the glory of God. David led Israel into a place of worship that the people of God had not known before.

We know that when God gave Moses the tabernacle, God told him to establish it and bring sacrifices, which are all types and symbols of Jesus Christ and His work. (See Exodus 25–31; 35–40.) They had feast days: Passover, Pentecost, Tabernacles. They had the sacrifices. They had the different rooms in which they would worship God. They would blow the shofar. They had priestly garments, incense, and the ark of God, or the ark of the covenant, which they placed behind the closed curtain—the veil—that separated the holy place from the most holy place. Only the high priest could go into the most holy place, once a year, with the blood of a lamb in order to make atonement on the mercy seat for the sins of the people. (See Leviticus 16.) But no one had access to the very presence and glory of God.

Because of sin, mankind was separated from God, so God introduced the people of Israel to sacrifices, atonement, and blood covering to atone for their sins yearly. They performed these ordinances on the Day of Atonement during the Feast of Tabernacles, and the priests would make atonement for all the sins of the people. But then something happened during the days of Samuel the prophet, before Israel had a king. Israel was fighting the Philistines and lost a battle, so they had an idea: "Let's bring the Ark of the Covenant of the LORD from Shiloh. If we carry it into battle with us, it will save us from our enemies" (1 Sam. 4:3, NLT).

But instead of winning the battle, they lost it, and they lost the ark too. The ark ended up in Philistia in the house of Dagon (1 Sam. 5:2). The Philistines had brought the ark as a trophy to their god. They put the ark of God next to the statue of Dagon. The next day, when the people of Ashdod woke up, they saw that Dagon had fallen forward on its face, breaking its hands (vv. 3–4). They were learning that no idol can stand in God's presence. So they stood the statue up again, but when they returned the next day, they saw it had fallen over again, and this time its neck had broken.

I don't know about you, but I wouldn't serve a god I had to pick up. I need a God who picks me up. I'd have left Dagon that day, saying, "If you have to pick him up, he ain't God. We don't need him." Aren't you glad that your God doesn't ever call you and say, "I need a pickup today"? You worship a God who picks you up.

NO MIXED OR COMPROMISED WORSHIP WILL DO

As one who speaks on behalf of heaven and uses their voice to bring heaven into situations, it is important to know whom you serve. It is important to know the truth that there is no other God beside Him. You will need high levels of discernment to know when something isn't God, to call it out and see deliverance come. This is how worship purifies our hearts and increases our awareness of God's glory. You cannot be a voice for God and not be a worshipper of God.

I was preaching in India some years ago, and we were praying for some people, when a young man came up. We began to pray for him, but we felt there was something blocking his deliverance. So we asked him, "Do you have any idols in your house?" We asked this because many in India are Hindus and therefore tend to worship many gods.

He said, "No, I don't. But my cousin needed a place to stay, and he brought his idols with him to the house."

We told him, "You must get those things out of your house, because they are demonic."

Then I thought about it. If a friend of mine didn't have a place to stay, and his idols said, "We need a place to stay too," he and his gods would be homeless! He cannot bring his broke gods into my home. I'm sorry.

Our God is rich and doesn't need us to put Him up for a few nights. He said, "If I were hungry, I would not tell you; for the world is Mine, and all its fullness" (Ps. 50:12, NKJV). He said, "Every beast of the forest is Mine, and the cattle on a thousand hills" (v. 10, NKJV). This is who we worship, and this is who the nations need to know is God. We cannot activate heaven on earth if we cannot discern the presence and glory of God—or the lack of it.

Back to the Philistines: God began to judge them. The Bible says that He "smote them with emerods" (1 Sam. 5:6). *Emerods* is another term for hemorrhoids.[1] The whole town got a bad case of hemorrhoids. And back then, they didn't have Preparation H or Tucks. There was no Walgreens or CVS.

They said, "We've got to get this thing out of here."

So they sent the ark of God back to Israel on a cart (1 Sam. 5:11; 6:1–12). When the people of Israel saw the cart coming, they rejoiced (v. 13). As we know, the ark of God represents God's presence. But it was not delivered into the land immediately. The people had become idol worshippers and needed to repent. They did, and God drove the Philistines out of their land. Over the next twenty years, the people would grow tired of Samuel and demand a king. Samuel would anoint Saul to be their first king. They would fight the Philistines again as well as other surrounding nations. Saul would disobey God and lose his throne to David.

BRINGING BACK THE ARK

Because of his love for the presence of God, David remembered the ark of the Lord and wanted to bring it to Jerusalem (1 Chron. 13). He knew he could not rule righteously without the presence of God. But bringing the ark into Jerusalem would not be easy, because once again some were disobedient. God had given the command that the ark was to be carried a certain way (Exod. 25:14–15), and the people had to keep a distance of one thousand yards between them and the ark (Josh. 3:4). The priest even covered it with three layers of cloth to keep people from seeing it (Num. 4:4–6, 15, 18–20). It housed the manifest glory of God.

But on this day, Uzzah thought he could keep the ark steady by holding it on the cart with his hand. He was wrong; he dropped dead the moment he touched it. The Bible says that "David was afraid of God that day, saying, 'How can I bring the ark of God to me?'" (1 Chron. 13:12, NKJV).

So they put it in the house of Obed-Edom, and it remained there for three months. Then the Bible says in 1 Chronicles 13:14 that God blessed the house of Obed-Edom. This is a revelation you can claim for yourself: when you get the presence of God in your house, you will be blessed. This is what you know as a worshipper. This is what you declare as a voice of heaven. You'll be blessed when God's presence is with you.

After the ark stayed for three months in the house of Obed-Edom, David went back to bring it to Zion. He didn't bring it back to the tabernacle of Moses, where it belonged. He brought it to Zion. David brought the ark of God to Jerusalem, set it under a tent, and established three courses of priests to worship twenty-four hours a day. (See 1 Chronicles 16:37–42; 25:1–6.) He appointed Levites to play instruments and praise God before the ark. Yet the ark of God, according to the Law of Moses, was intended to be in the holy of holies behind the curtain, which was in Shiloh (Gen. 49:10; Josh. 1:8).

I often wonder what led David to bring the ark to Zion and put it under a tent. I don't believe that he, as a prophet of God, did it without God inspiring him to do it. I believe God gave David foresight into something called the kingdom age, a time when the ark of God would no longer be behind a curtain, a time when God's people would have access to the presence of God in praise and worship.

David established this atmosphere of open praise and worship with the help of three prophetic families: the families of Asaph, Heman, and Jeduthun. (See 1 Chronicles 25:1–6.) Each of them had sons and daughters who prophesied with musical instruments, and David told them to do this twenty-four hours a day. Each of the families took an eight-hour shift, and on a rotating schedule they worshipped and praised before the ark of God twenty-four hours a day, seven days a week. The Scripture actually uses the term *prophesy*: "Moreover David and the captains of the army separated for the service some of the sons of Asaph, of Heman, and of Jeduthun, who should prophesy with harps, stringed instruments, and cymbals" (1 Chron. 25:1, NKJV). They were not told to just play. They were told to prophesy with the instruments.

MORE THAN A SONG

This is where we see that David established not just worship but prophetic worship. David shows us that worshipping God has always been more than just singing songs. It's something done by the unction of the Holy Ghost. It's something done by the anointing of God. It's something that we carry as we use our voices to proclaim the kingdom and the nature and character of God. It's something that comes when the Spirit of God comes upon you. Jesus in John 4 tells the woman at the well that the day is coming when men who worship God must worship Him in spirit and truth. (See John 4:23.)

Of course, He was referring to the day when the Spirit of God would be poured out on the day of Pentecost and the sons and daughters would prophesy. So when God baptizes you in the Holy Ghost—when the Spirit of God comes upon you—it's so you can do more than speak in tongues. It's giving you the ability to worship God in a way you've never worshipped before. It's putting something prophetic on your life so you can become a worshipper. Your worship is your voice, and your voice your worship.

God didn't fill you with the Holy Ghost so you can try to impress people with how much you speak in tongues. God filled you with the Holy Ghost to make you a worshipper, because He knew that in order to really satisfy God, you would need to know what pleases Him.

How do we know what God wants? How do we know the songs God wants us to sing, the words He wants us to speak, the prayers He wants us to pray, the assignments He wants us to complete, and the lives He wants us to touch? How do we know what to offer God? Because let me tell you something: God doesn't just accept anything. We think we can just come to church and throw anything up to Him. We think that we can do this thing or the other and say that God approves of it, but He is very particular about what He accepts.

WORSHIP GOD ACCEPTS

Did you know that God rejects things? If you've been taught that God doesn't reject anybody, you need to read about King Saul. God told Samuel, "Stop praying, for I've rejected him. I found a man after My own heart." (See 1 Samuel 16:1.) Read about Cain; God rejected his offering. I talk about this more in my book *Destroying the Spirit of Rejection*. The bottom line is God doesn't accept just anything.

You can't give just anything to God and say, "Here, God. Take it. Here's Your worship. Here are my plans. Here's my offering." Too many people who have good incomes show up at the altar with a one-dollar bill that is folded so tight the deacon has to use a crowbar to get it open when the money is counted. They just drop anything in the offering bucket without giving some thought to what would be equal to our giving God our best.

Sticking with the giving analogy, because worship includes how we give, some of us know we can spend one hundred dollars, two hundred dollars, even three hundred dollars on hair, nails, shoes, a bag, or a pedicure. But when we get to church and the preacher says, "Come and bless the Lord," we're digging out one-dollar bills. Now, if that's all you have, that's a different story. Some of us have more but don't take offering seriously.

God gives you His best. He gave you His best when He gave you Jesus. You ought to give Him your best. Don't just give God anything. That will never work if you want to approach God with a true heart of worship.

A favorite Scripture passage many Christians like to fall back on is the story of the widow's mite. (See Mark 12:41–44 and Luke 21:1–4.) The difference here is that not many of us are widows. We are not in the same socioeconomic situation as she was, so her ability was different than our ability. She gave all. Are you giving all?

DISCERNING WHAT GOD WANTS

Being prophetic means more than being able to deliver a string of words that carry a certain sound and cause people to jump and shout. Prophets have the ability to know what God likes and doesn't like. They just know it by His Spirit. They have an unction. That's why if you're prophetic and you're in certain ministries, you feel nothing during the worship time. You will see people running and falling out, and think, "Are you kidding me? There is no glory here. This is flesh." Prophetic people know, and you can know, as you are prophetic as well.

Most often, when you have spent enough time with God and gotten to know Him and His presence, you will more often know when something isn't God than when it is. For example, when a false prophet shows up and begins to prophesy, you will sense something isn't right. Again, people may be falling out or shaking, but you will feel that something is not right. You know you are thinking and feeling differently than those around you. You can sense all kinds of devils in the room: Leviathan, Jezebel, witchcraft, lust, and perversion.

As a voice of heaven you have an unction, a fervor, a fire of holiness that alerts you when something's not right. You are grieved. You are vexed. You may try to shake it and just go along with the program for a while, but like your heavenly Father, you can't just accept or be party to anything. You may even spend time praying about it. That something you feel is called discernment.

It's what you develop as you draw closer to God, and it becomes sharper the more you become like Him. The more you become like Him, the more you will come to love the things He loves and hate the things He hates.

Everything can look right on the outside, because believers are good at being religious in church. We know how to have church. We know how to sing. We know how to do it all. Many of us have been doing it for years. Everything looks right and sounds right; everybody is up smiling.

Where pure worship happens is not a matter of being Baptist, Methodist, Catholic, Church of God, Charismatic, or Pentecostal. It's none of that. True worship is in spirit and truth. I've been in Baptist churches where I felt the anointing and then went to a Pentecostal church and felt nothing. Worship that pleases God has nothing to do with denomination. It depends on the heart. It depends on the people. I don't go by what's on the door. I'm looking for the anointing of God. I'm looking for the glory of God. I'm not looking for who the bishop is, who the pastor is, or how nice the building looks. Those things make no difference to God, and they make no difference to me.

WHEN GOD IS PLEASED

Some time ago I was in Cologne, Germany, preaching. Cologne has the largest Gothic cathedral in Europe. When you drive into Cologne, the huge cathedral is one of the sites you cannot miss. It dominates the skyline. It took 632 years for construction to be completed—and you thought your church building program was long. When you go into a cathedral, it's huge, dark, and filled with the tombs of bishops and cardinals. Can you imagine trying to get your worship on with a tomb next to you?

Of course, it's a Catholic cathedral, and they have been praying, singing, and worshipping in the same way for about as long as it took to build the cathedral. I do not say this to mock anyone's worship. Jesus said they that worship God must worship Him in spirit and in truth (John 4:24), so as we talk about activating your voice through worship, we're not just talking about prophesying. We're talking about the worship you engage in that brings you into a place where God's presence becomes your dwelling place. While He inhabits your praises (Ps. 22:3), you sit and gaze at the beauty of the Lord and inquire in His temple (Ps. 27:4).

Worship is where the exchange happens and God tells you great and mighty things you don't know (Jer. 33:3)—solutions to problems, innovative strategies, witty inventions, book ideas, and so much more. Worship is where you declare the glory of God in everything you say and do.

And it should be a transformative experience, where the Spirit of God moves you in and out of the flow of what He is doing in your life and in the areas to which He's called you. From season to season He is always doing new things. Growing in your ability to discern what He is doing is critical to your call. That is why rote worship can be very limiting.

I'm not against singing songs that we learned, because God does anoint songs, and there are some great songs being sung in churches. But there comes a time when we need to be in the welcoming atmosphere of prophetic worship that is full of the Holy Ghost, because it stirs up the gift of God inside us. David set up a pattern for worship. That did not make him perfect, but it did cause God to call him a man after His heart. He set up those three families. He looked for some prophetic people who knew how to flow in the Holy Ghost. Not just anybody—he looked for some Asaphs, Hemans, and Jeduthuns because he wanted to give God the best. David, a prophet, knew what God wanted, so he established something that had never been established in Israel—twenty-four-hour worship, prophets, and prophesying. What is God leading you to establish?

Your gifts and your calling cannot thrive in a worship environment where people can just sing really well but don't have a holy lifestyle. No, you need to be surrounded by people who are full of the Holy Ghost and are prophetic. This is the atmosphere that activates and stirs your ability to hear and know what God wants to release through you. True prophetic worship builds such a love and desire for the things of God that you will simply ask, "God, what do You want? What kind of praise do You want? What kind of worship do You want? What do You want me to offer You, God? What do You desire me to say in this hour?"

This is not about a service or a denomination. This is not about a hymnal. This is about God. Activating your voice is not about you walking around prophesying to everybody. It's not about you walking around trying to discern what's in everybody's heart and trying to find their sin. It's about you knowing and doing what God wants, what pleases Him. And you will walk in this knowledge not because you're smarter than anyone else, but because God has given you an unction, a gift to know when repentance is needed, when prayer is needed, when fasting is needed. You will know when a word of correction is needed and when the Spirit of God is grieved. You will know when God is happy and pleased, and by your words you will be able to lead people into a place where they are aligned with God too.

ACTIVATING YOUR VOICE

If you've followed my ministry for any amount of time, attended a service at Crusaders Church, or heard me speak at a conference, then you are familiar with my use of prayers, decrees, and declarations at the end of my messages. I use this pattern in my books as well. When we speak the word we have been exposed to in a message or that resulted from a personal revelation from God, another level of faith is activated in us, and what we have heard takes root in our lives. With greater faith, there is a greater level of manifestation.

We have the power to create with our words, just as our Father God does. He spoke, and it was so. We speak, and it is so. Our world has been and is shaped by words.

We have the power to speak life or death; we have the power to speak things that were not as though they were. This is why it is so important that we understand not only how we activate heaven with our words but also that we are indeed the heavens as Paul revealed. So as we have come to this point in the book, where we've understood another aspect of our identity in Christ, how to answer the call, in what ways the call to "preach" can be manifested, and the purity and virtue of heaven's voice, it is time to be activated.

In my book *Prophetic Activation*, I go into depth about the power and practice of activation, especially in relation to spiritual gifts specific to prophesying. As you speak, you are first hearing from God what to relay or minister to people, whether at home, in corporate America, or in the nations. What I explain is that to activate something is to start it off, trigger it, or set it in motion. Activations are spiritual exercises that use words, actions, phrases, objects, Scripture verses, worship songs, dance, prophetic prayers, and more to trigger the prophetic gifts and help believers in every area of life and ministry to flow freely as they are commissioned to release God's Word in the earth. You've already experienced a few of these as you read earlier chapters.

Activations set in motion prophetic utterances, songs, and movement that will bring great blessing to the members of local churches, ministries, and the world.

Activations are designed to break down the barriers that prevent people from operating in prophecy. These barriers include fear, doubt, timidity, and ignorance. This will also provide people an opportunity to minister, some for the first time, in a safe and loving environment.

Activations rekindle and fan the flame of ministries that have become stagnant in the prophetic flow. We all need times of rekindling and reigniting. Prophetic activations will ignite believers and churches to prophesy. Motionless churches need to be set in motion. Prophetic activations can get us moving again.

> That is why I would remind you to stir up (rekindle the embers of, fan the flame of, and keep burning) the [gracious] gift of God, [the inner fire] that is in you by means of the laying on of my hands [with those of the elders at your ordination].
>
> —2 TIMOTHY 1:6, AMPC

The value of different activations is that they will break your limitations and give you the ability to operate in different ways. Don't be limited to your favorite way, but be ready to move in different ways and administrations. Your expression of gifts must never become boring and routine but should always be exciting and new. God has many surprises for us, and the prophetic will always release new things.

Activations are not designed to make everyone a prophet—only God can call and commission a prophet. Activations are simply designed to stir people to grow in whatever level they are called to. There may be people participating and leading activations who are prophets, some who have the gift of prophecy, and some who have the spirit of prophecy as a result of being filled with the Holy Ghost. But there also may be people in the activations who are psalmists, minstrels, intercessors, counselors, preachers, teachers, and dancers. Activations will stir them and cause them to move more in faith and inspiration. The following decrees are designed to do just that.

DECREES THAT RELEASE HEAVEN'S VOICE

Lord, give me strength to bring forth my destiny as heaven's voice (Isa. 66:9).

Lord, let me not operate in the wrong spirit (Luke 9:55).

Let me have and walk in an excellent spirit (Dan. 6:3).

Lord, stir up my spirit to do Your will (Hag. 1:14).

I reject all false prophetic ministry, in the name of Jesus (2 Pet. 2:1).

_____

I reject the mouth of vanity and the right hand of falsehood (Ps. 144:8).

_____

I reject every false vision and every false prophetic word released into my life (Jer. 14:14).

_____

I bind Satan, the deceiver, from releasing any deception into my life (Rev. 12:9).

_____

I bind and cast out all spirits of self-deception, in the name of Jesus (1 Cor. 3:18).

_____

I bind and cast out any spirit of sorcery that would deceive me, in the name of Jesus (Rev. 18:23).

_____

Lord, let no man deceive me (Matt. 24:4).

_____

I bind and rebuke any bewitchment that would keep me from obeying the truth (Gal. 3:1).

_____

I pray for utterance and boldness to make known the mystery of the gospel (Eph. 6:19).

I bind and cast out any spirit of Absalom that would try to steal my heart from God's ordained leadership (2 Sam. 15:6).

_____

Lord, cleanse my life from secret faults (Ps. 19:12).

_____

Lord, let Your secret be upon my tabernacle (Job 29:4).

_____

Lead me and guide me for Your name's sake (Ps. 31:3).

_____

Guide me continually (Isa. 58:11).

_____

Guide me into all truth (John 16:13).

_____

Guide me with Your eye (Ps. 32:8).

_____

Let me guide my affairs with discretion (Ps. 112:5).

_____

Guide me by the skillfulness of Your hands (Ps. 78:72).

_____

Lead me in a plain path, because of my enemies (Ps. 27:11).

Lead me not into temptation, but deliver me from evil (Matt. 6:13).

_____

Lead me, and make Your way straight before my eyes (Ps. 5:8).

_____

Make the crooked places straight and the rough places smooth before me (Isa. 40:4).

_____

Send out Your light and truth, and let them lead me (Ps. 43:3).

_____

Make darkness light before me and crooked things straight (Isa. 42:16).

_____

Lord, give me wisdom in every area where I lack (Jas. 1:5).

PRAYERS THAT RELEASE REVELATION

You are a God that reveals secrets. Lord, reveal Your secrets unto me (Dan. 2:28).

_____

Reveal to me the secret and deep things (Dan. 2:22).

Let me understand things kept secret from the foundation of the world (Matt. 13:35).

_____

Let the seals be broken from Your Word (Dan. 12:9).

_____

Let me understand and have revelation of Your will and purpose (Col. 1:9).

_____

Give me the spirit of wisdom and revelation, and let the eyes of my understanding be enlightened (Eph. 1:17–18).

_____

Let me understand heavenly things (John 3:12).

_____

Open my eyes to behold wondrous things out of Your Word (Ps. 119:18).

_____

Let me know and understand the mysteries of the kingdom (Mark 4:11).

_____

Let me speak to others by revelation (1 Cor. 14:6).

_____

Reveal Your secrets to Your servants the prophets (Amos 3:7).

Let the hidden things be made manifest (Mark 4:22).

_____

Hide Your truths from the wise and prudent, and reveal them to babes (Matt. 11:25).

_____

Let Your arm be revealed in my life (John 12:38).

_____

Reveal the things that belong to me (Deut. 29:29).

_____

Let Your Word be revealed unto me (1 Sam. 3:7).

_____

Let Your glory be revealed in my life (Isa. 40:5).

_____

Let Your righteousness be revealed in my life (Isa. 56:1).

_____

Let me receive visions and revelations of the Lord (2 Cor. 12:1).

_____

Let me receive an abundance of revelations (2 Cor. 12:7).

_____

Let me be a good steward of Your revelations (1 Cor. 4:1).

Let me speak the mystery of Christ (Col. 4:3).

_____

Let me receive and understand Your hidden wisdom (1 Cor. 2:7).

_____

Hide not Your commandments from me (Ps. 119:19).

_____

Let me speak the wisdom of God in a mystery (1 Cor. 2:7).

_____

Let me make known the mystery of the gospel (Eph. 6:19).

_____

Make known unto me the mystery of Your will (Eph. 1:9).

_____

Open Your dark sayings upon the harp (Ps. 49:4).

_____

Let me understand Your parables; the words of the wise and their dark sayings (Prov. 1:6).

_____

Lord, lighten my candle and enlighten my darkness (Ps. 18:28).

_____

Make darkness light before me (Isa. 42:16).

Give me the treasures of darkness and hidden riches in secret places (Isa. 45:3).

_____

Let Your candle shine upon my head (Job 29:3).

_____

My spirit is the candle of the Lord, searching all the inward parts of the belly (Prov. 20:27).

_____

Let me understand the deep things of God (1 Cor. 2:10).

_____

Let me understand Your deep thoughts (Ps. 92:5).

_____

Let my eyes be enlightened with Your Word (Ps. 19:8).

_____

My eyes are blessed to see (Luke 10:23).

_____

Let all spiritual cataracts and scales be removed from my eyes (Acts 9:18).

_____

Let me comprehend with all saints what is the breadth and length and depth and height of Your love that I may speak it and minister it to those I am called to (Eph. 3:18).

CHAPTER 9

LET IT BE HEARD— RELEASE YOUR VOICE

*Whatever I speak, just as the Father
has told Me, so I speak.*
—JOHN 12:50, NKJV

I N CHAPTER 6 of my book *Prophet, Arise!* I talk about the prophet Jonah. In the first three verses of the Book of Jonah, he typifies what I have coined as "Jonah prophets on the run." These are people whom God calls to speak His words in the earth to a specific need, cause, or people, but for various reasons they try to avoid delivering the word and find ways to hide from God. Let's revisit these verses, and then I will share more about how this story ties into your voice:

Now the word of the LORD came to Jonah the son of Amittai, saying, "Arise, go to Nineveh, that great city, and cry out against it; for their wickedness has come up before Me."
But Jonah arose to flee to Tarshish from the presence

of the LORD. He went down to Joppa, and found a ship going to Tarshish; so he paid the fare, and went down into it, to go with them to Tarshish from the presence of the LORD.

—JONAH 1:1–3, NKJV

So Jonah was a prophet on the run. He was running away from the assignment God gave him to go to Nineveh and tell them to repent. He didn't want to deliver the message God told him to deliver because he felt that if he told them to repent, they would. Nineveh was a city in Assyria, and the Assyrians were mortal enemies of Israel. Therefore, Jonah did not like the Ninevites and wanted judgment to come on them. So unlike what we may think of prophets and their desire to see people turn their lives around, Jonah hoped it would go the other way for the Ninevites, that they would indeed not repent and be burned up. When they did repent, he actually complained to God about it:

Ah, LORD, was not this what I said when I was still in my country? Therefore I fled previously to Tarshish; for I know that You are a gracious and merciful God, slow to anger and abundant in lovingkindness, One who relents from doing harm. Therefore now, O LORD, please take my life from me, for it is better for me to die than to live!

—JONAH 4:2–3, NKJV

Yes, Jonah was really going through it. What this shows us is that sometimes even the called or sought-out ones can have people issues they have not dealt with. We talked about this in chapter 7, how important it is to have long-suffering. Jonah was not long-suffering, and yet God gave him a word to go to Nineveh. Instead of obeying, he fled the presence of the Lord and went to Tarshish. And I have already sort of given you the spoiler: Jonah gave the word after being thrown overboard the ship he boarded to go to Tarshish. God had caused a terrible storm to come, and the only way for the people on the boat to be saved was to throw Jonah over the side. Jonah was then swallowed by a great fish and stayed there for three days until the fish spat him out on the shore of Nineveh. Jonah could not outrun God, so he went and delivered the message to the people, and they repented and were saved from God's wrath.

So if you've made it to this chapter in the book—you know you have a call, an assignment to use your voice to speak heaven into the earth; you've read and studied; you've been imparted into and commissioned but still are not preaching and proclaiming heaven—this is a word for you: stop running from your assignment. Don't be like Jonah, trying to run from God. You know you can't outrun Him. What storms and big fish has He put in your way to get you back on track with your assignment? If you will just obey, that thing will spit you out, and you will be able to complete your assignment.

There are many people who really draw back from their calling or anointing. It intimidates them. They run from it. They don't like it. They don't like what they see concerning it. They don't like what they hear. And sometimes, they don't necessarily like the gift itself. So they run from the calling. But many of them will come into their calling, obey God, and do what God has called them to do as they discover more about it, as they come under the right leadership to mentor and coach them, and as they are activated by reading and studying, pressing in to God instead of running away.

This book was written to stir you, to cause you to rise up

in obedience to inspiration. It was designed to move you forward past your fears, your doubts, or whatever tries to keep you from being the voice God has called you to be.

STOP RUNNING

Are you running away from your assignment to speak the word of the Lord, to speak heaven into the earth? Are you running from the presence of the Lord? Are you hiding? The Lord is calling you, yet you will not be the first, and you will not be the last. There are Jonahs in every generation. There are Jonahs running from God today. Don't be a prophet on the run. Be the one who answers the call of God. Be the one who will use his or her voice to deliver, heal, and set free. You have been called to bless your generation. Don't run and hide from the call; embrace it and obey God today.

If you are one who is rebelling against or fearing what it means to speak for the Lord, I pray that His word in your heart will be like fire shut up in your bones. In Jeremiah 20:9 the prophet Jeremiah wrote about how he got so angry that he did not want to speak the word of the Lord anymore because of all the opposition he received from being a voice for the Lord. He said he tried to stop, but the word was like fire shut up in his bones, and he could not contain himself. He had to give the word of the Lord.

There are many people who say, "I'm not going to speak for God because there's too much opposition, too much persecution. If I say this or that, I will be rejected, cancelled, and forgotten. I don't want that to happen to me, so I'm just going to shut up and be quiet."

But when the word of the Lord is stirred inside of you, you

will become like Jeremiah, who said, "His word was in me, like fire shut up in my bones."

You cannot hide from God. You cannot hide in the bottom of a ship as Jonah did. You cannot hide from the presence of the Lord. You must arise and go to the place or people God is calling you to. When you go and preach the word of the Lord in the way only you can, the results will be astonishing, just as they were for Jonah. In his story, the whole city repented and was spared. Can you imagine? A whole city was spared from judgment because one person finally obeyed God.

YOUR VOICE CAN SAVE A GENERATION

The call of God can save a generation. The call of God can save families and individuals. Your calling is important. God has an assignment for you. God has a word He wants to put inside of you, and it's not just for you; it's for your generation. When you obey that word, when you answer the call, you bring salvation, blessing, and deliverance to people God sends you to—and even to those you may not like.

What if they don't listen? Whether or not they receive you and how God has called you to serve them, whether they receive the word or ministry you have brought to them, that is between them and God. The Book of Ezekiel says this:

> When I say to the wicked, "You shall surely die," and you give him no warning, nor speak to warn the wicked from his wicked way, to save his life, that same wicked man shall die in his iniquity; but his blood I will require at your hand. Yet, if you warn the wicked, and he does not turn from his wickedness, nor from his wicked way, he shall die in his iniquity; but you have delivered your soul.
> —Ezekiel 3:18–19, NKJV

So, yes, there may be those who reject what God has sent you to say or do on His behalf, and they may end up being judged, but those who do receive it, God will save and deliver. Don't run from your assignment to be and do all God has called you to be and do. Embrace it and obey Him, and He will take care of the rest.

USE YOUR VOICE TO ACTIVATE THE RULE OF GOD IN YOUR FINANCES

Within the last few years, I attended a conference called the Fearless Voice. It was put on by my friends LaJun and Valora Cole, who have a ministry based in Tampa, Florida. I had never been to a conference called Fearless Voice. What a unique name. What a unique vision. At the time of this writing, we are beginning a new decade—not another year, another decade. And I want you to believe that God causes you to supernaturally see some things you've never seen before.

Get ready. Begin to set your course not only for what's coming up in the next few days, month, or even this year but for all that will come in the next ten years. Don't limit God. Believe Him for something supernatural to hit your life, health, business, ministry, finances, and relationships. Prospering in all areas of life is part of the blessing of the shalom (peace) that comes from walking in covenant with God and coming into agreement with heaven.

I believe in wealth and prosperity. I do. Those who say money can't make you happy must have never had any. Money is not our master, of course. God is. Having money and the wisdom of God regarding how to use it is where peace and prosperity reign. So we understand that. Now, what is true is that having financial difficulty and being broke surely don't make you happy.

God wants you to enjoy life and have more than enough. Wealth, riches, and joy are gifts from God. Ecclesiastes 5:19 says God gives wealth, riches, and joy, which points back to Proverbs 10:22: "The blessing of the LORD makes one rich, and He adds no sorrow with it" (NKJV). You can have money and enjoy it. You can be happy and enjoy life. You can do what you want to do, go where you want to go, give what you want to give, bless who you want to bless, sponsor who you want to sponsor—and get joy out of doing so.

I want you to believe God that this is you. I want you to declare and know that when you open your mouth, heaven is speaking. And so, I am going to challenge you to use your voice to speak over your finances. Declare and let heaven speak. Let the rule of God be released through your voice and over your finances no matter what your financial situation is right now. The Bible says that you can decree a thing, and it shall be established (Job 22:28). Open your mouth and speak over your money, bank accounts, investments, real estate. Maybe even as you are reading this, you have some opportunities or deals waiting to be closed, and opposition is set against you. They don't want to give it to you even though you have the money to buy it. They are trying to price you out. Say aloud right now, "I can't be priced out. I will not be priced out." Now pray this prayer with me.

> *Lord, I open my mouth over my finances and over my giving. I speak wealth; riches; prosperity; abundance; favor; more than enough; increase; multiplication to my finances, my bank account, my savings, and my*

*investments. Thank You, Lord, that as I speak now
as an oracle of God, I release the rule of heaven over
my money. I refuse all poverty or lack, in the name
of Jesus. My finances will increase more and more
in the days to come. I will have more than I need,
more than enough, in the name of Jesus. The seeds of
giving I sow will multiply. I will reap bountifully. A
bountiful harvest is coming into my life. I will enjoy
a good harvest in the good land, in the name of Jesus.
Thank You, Lord. This is Your word that comes out
of my mouth, and it is being established in my life. I
decree it, in Jesus' name. Amen.*

LET HEAVEN'S VOICE BE HEARD

As you come to understand this new expression of your identity in Christ, this position of being the heavens Paul and the
psalmist spoke about, of being one who declares the glory
of God, of one who by their words and actions loose in the
earth the things that are loosed in heaven, an anointing and
unction are going to arise within you. The word of the Lord
and the fire of compassion for broken people will move you
to preach like you've never preached before; to prophesy on
another level; to sing like you've never sung before; to pray
and intercede, to minister healing, and to seek solutions all
like you never have before. Your workplace, church, or com-
munity will get a new you. They will encounter one who sits
in heavenly places and lives his or her life from this reality.

You will begin to speak in other tongues like you've never
spoken before. God is about to put a new anointing on your

mouth, on your lips, and on your voice. I prophesy it right now in the name of Jesus.

When you open your mouth, get ready for miracle after miracle after miracle to come from what you speak. Even when you don't feel like preaching, your life will be a sermon. God is calling you out and saying, "Preach!" Be instant in season and out of season. When the devil comes against you, preach harder, preach stronger, and preach longer.

Declare right now: "Devil, you can't shut my mouth. God has anointed my words. I will open my mouth. I will say it. I will decree it."

I want to challenge you to get ready for open doors and new places where you've never preached before. Be ready for your line to go out into all the earth. You will be sought out. They will call you up. A Macedonian call is coming upon your life. "Come over to Macedonia," they will say, "we need you."

NEW VOICES

As God spoke to me about this other aspect of our identity in Him, He confirmed to me that not only will your voice be loosed, but He is also going to raise up the voices of your sons and daughters. Your grandchildren are going to preach and prophesy. Another generation of voices is arising.

I close out this book looking forward to our present and future generations experiencing Joel 2:28 moments more frequently, where old men will dream dreams and young men will see visions, where our sons and daughters will prophesy, bringing heaven to earth.

The world needs us to be who God has called us to be, and for some of you, the enemy has attacked your voice not just spiritually but also naturally. Some of you have felt so discouraged. You have felt as if your voice really doesn't make a difference. "No one listens to me anyway," you may have repeated to yourself. Or, "I don't have a platform. I don't have a stage. I don't have a pulpit. I don't have a microphone. My voice is not important." The Lord wants to release you and your voice into a new place.

I believe the Lord gave me this word, *Activate Heaven*, to cause you to see what God says about heaven speaking and you being the heavens. I believe He wants you to know that just as there is no place off limits to His voice, there is no place off limits to your voice.

Let God do His miracles. The world needs your voice. The body of Christ needs your voice. Your voice is one of the most important things God has given you.

The enemy wants to shut doors on you, but God says, "I'm opening doors no man can shut." Open your mouth and activate heaven.

PRAYER TO RELEASE HEAVEN ON EARTH

Thank You, Lord, for releasing heaven on earth. Let heaven speak. Let heaven's voice be heard in every place, every region, every city, every house. Let the voice of heaven be heard, in the name of Jesus, on the streets, on the street corners, in the dope houses, in the prostitution houses. Lord, wherever Your voice needs to go, let it go, in the name of Jesus. I believe for a release of Your voice to be heard in every way that brings healing, blessing, and deliverance. Amen.

PRAYER AGAINST PHYSICAL ATTACKS ON YOUR VOICE

Father, as an apostle of God, I take authority over every assignment of hell that comes against your voice. I speak healing over your vocal cords. I come against laryngitis, hoarseness, losing your voice, and not being able to speak. I come against this in the name of Jesus.

I rebuke that spirit of infirmity, those spirits that attack your voice at night. Let your vocal cords be loosened in the name of Jesus. I pray that the singer's vocal cords be loosened.

I come against demons that make you want to stutter when you go to speak. Demons that make you feel like you can't get the words out or that cause you to be confused about what you need to say, come out in the name of Jesus. Loose them and go!

I come against dumb spirits that keep you from speaking and preaching.

I come against the spirit that causes fear to grab you when you go to speak, the spirit that causes you to be afraid to get up in front of people. I command that demon of fear to come out, in the name of Jesus.

Demons that attack the ears, throat, tonsils, tongue, sinuses, mouth, chest, lungs, and heart, come out. Go, in the name of Jesus, loose and come out now.

I come against every assignment of witchcraft that comes to attack your voice. I come against witches and warlocks speaking against your ministry. Sorcery, go. Divination and witchcraft, loose.

I decree healing over your voice, voice box, and vocal cords in the name of Jesus. I decree supernatural grace and anointing over your voice in the name of Jesus.

DECLARATIONS TO LOOSE YOURSELF FROM SPIRITUAL WEAPONS THAT FORM AGAINST YOUR VOICE

I loose myself from every assignment of witchcraft sent to attack my voice.

I break every spoken curse from witches, warlocks, and sorcerers that comes against my word, my message, and my voice. I loose myself. No weapon formed against me shall prosper, in the name of Jesus. I will speak. I will have a voice, in the name of Jesus.

I will not lose my voice. I will have a strong voice, in the name of Jesus.

NOTES

INTRODUCTION

1. Blue Letter Bible, s.v. "*kēryssō*," accessed September 7, 2020, https://www.blueletterbible.org/lang/lexicon/lexicon. cfm?Strongs=G2784&t=KJV.
2. Blue Letter Bible, s.v. "*praus*," accessed September 7, 2020, https://www.blueletterbible.org/lang/lexicon/lexicon. cfm?Strongs=G4239&t=KJV.
3. Guy Duininck, *Grace for Effectual Ministry* (N.p.: Master's Touch Ministries, 2001), as quoted on TonyCooke.org, "Grace for Effectual Ministry—Locating, Cultivating, and Using Your Spiritual Giftings," tonycooke.org/articles-by-others/grace-effectual-ministry/.
4. Bible Hub, s.v. "Matthew 3:4," accessed September 7, 2020, https://biblehub.com/commentaries/matthew/3-4.htm.

CHAPTER 1

1. Blue Letter Bible, s.v. "*qav*," accessed September 7, 2020, https://www.blueletterbible.org/lang/Lexicon/Lexicon. cfm?strongs=H6957&t=KJV.
2. Blue Letter Bible, s.v. "*phthongos*," accessed September 7, 2020, https://www.blueletterbible.org/lang/lexicon/lexicon. cfm?Strongs=G5353&t=KJV.
3. Blue Letter Bible, s.v. "*phthongos*," accessed September 7, 2020, https://www.blueletterbible.org/lang/Lexicon/Lexicon. cfm?strongs=G5353&t=KJV. See Thayer's Greek Lexicon.

4. Martin G. Collins, "What the Bible Says About Sea as a Symbol," Forerunner Commentary, accessed September 7, 2020, https://www.bibletools.org/index.cfm/fuseaction/Topical. show/RTD/cgg/ID/4342/Sea-as-Symbol.htm.

CHAPTER 2

1. Blue Letter Bible, s.v. "*tsaba'*," accessed September 7, 2020, https://www.blueletterbible.org/lang/Lexicon/Lexicon. cfm?strongs=H6635&t=KJV.
2. See, for instance, the Contemporary English Version, the Good News Translation, the New American Standard Bible, and the New International Version.

CHAPTER 3

1. See 2 Timothy 3:16 in the AMP, ESV, and NIV.
2. Blue Letter Bible, s.v. "*pneuma*," accessed September 7, 2020, https://www.blueletterbible.org/lang/lexicon/lexicon. cfm?Strongs=G4151&t=KJV.

CHAPTER 4

1. James Ellsmoor, "Smart Cities: The Future of Urban Development," Forbes, May 19, 2019, https://www.forbes.com/ sites/jamesellsmoor/2019/05/19/smart-cities-the-future-of-urban-development/#2394ef9a2f90.
2. Kevin Helms, "Akon City: $6 Billion Cryptocurrency City Set to Begin Construction," BitCoin, June 20, 2020, https://news. bitcoin.com/akon-city-akoin-cryptocurrency/.
3. Union of International Associations Nations, *The Encyclopedia of World Problems and Human Potential*, accessed September 7, 2020, https://uia.org/encyclopedia.

CHAPTER 5

1. Blue Letter Bible, s.v. "*hyparchonta*," accessed September 7, 2020, https://www.blueletterbible.org/lang/lexicon/lexicon. cfm?Strongs=G5224&t=KJV.

2."Remembering Andraé Crouch," HomecomingMagazine.com, April 1, 2015, http://www.homecomingmagazine.com/article/ remembering-andra-crouch/.

CHAPTER 6

1. Webster's Dictionary 1828, s.v. "virtue," accessed September 7, 2020, http://webstersdictionary1828.com/Dictionary/virtue.

2. Art Katz, "Virtue, Power and Healing," Art Katz Ministries, accessed September 7, 2020, http://artkatzministries.org/ articles/virtue-power-and-healing/.

3. Katz, "Virtue, Power and Healing."

4. Katz, "Virtue, Power and Healing."

5. Larry Ellis, "Real Beauty," *Larry's Stuff* (blog), accessed September 7, 2020, http://www.larryssermonblog. com/414794071.

6. *Merriam-Webster* (thesaurus), s.v. "virtue," accessed September 7, 2020, https://www.merriam-webster.com/ thesaurus/virtue.

7. Webster's Dictionary 1828, s.v. "humility," accessed September 7, 2020, http://webstersdictionary1828.com/Dictionary/ humility.

8."Saint Augustine Quotes," BrainyQuote.com, accessed September 7, 2020, https://www.brainyquote.com/quotes/saint_ augustine_124552.

9. Donald DeMarco, *The Heart of Virtue* (San Francisco: Ignatius Press, 2017), https://books.google.com/ books?id=IIgme3rPSYEC.

10. Webster's Dictionary 1828, s.v. "meekness," accessed September 7, 2020, http://webstersdictionary1828.com/Dictionary/meekness.

11. "25 Virtues Found in the Best of Men," Quizlet, Inc., accessed September 7, 2020, https://quizlet.com/406173400/25-virtues-found-in-the-best-of-men-flash-cards/.

12. Webster's Dictionary 1828, s.v. "generosity," accessed September 7, 2020, http://webstersdictionary1828.com/Dictionary/generosity.

13. Webster's Dictionary 1828, s.v. "courage," accessed September 7, 2020, http://webstersdictionary1828.com/Dictionary/courage.

14. Jena McGregor, "Maya Angelou on Leadership, Courage, and the Creative Process," *Washington Post*, May 28, 2014, https://www.washingtonpost.com/news/on-leadership/wp/2014/05/28/maya-angelou-on-leadership-courage-and-the-creative-process/.

15. Webster's Dictionary 1828, s.v. "frugality," accessed September 7, 2020, http://webstersdictionary1828.com/Dictionary/frugality.

16. Webster's Dictionary 1828, s.v. "temperance," accessed September 7, 2020, http://webstersdictionary1828.com/Dictionary/temperance.

17. Webster's Dictionary 1828, s.v. "kindness," accessed September 7, 2020, http://webstersdictionary1828.com/Dictionary/kindness.

18. Webster's Dictionary 1828, s.v. "patience," accessed September 7, 2020, http://webstersdictionary1828.com/Dictionary/patience.

19. Webster's Dictionary 1828, s.v. "fortitude," accessed September 7, 2020, http://webstersdictionary1828.com/Dictionary/Fortitude.

20. Webster's Dictionary 1828, s.v. "fortitude."

21. Webster's Dictionary 1828, s.v. "stedfastness," accessed September 7, 2020, http://webstersdictionary1828.com/Dictionary/stedfastness.

22. Aly McCarthy, "What Are the 40 Virtues?" Families of Character, March 21, 2018, https://www.familiesofcharacter. com/devblog10809/2018/3/21/what-are-the-40-virtues-full-list.
23. McCarthy, "What Are the 40 Virtues?"
24. McCarthy, "What Are the 40 Virtues?"
25. Webster's Dictionary 1828, s.v. "compassion," accessed September 7, 2020, http://webstersdictionary1828.com/ Dictionary/compassion.
26. Webster's Dictionary 1828, s.v. "compassion."
27. StudyBlue, "Virtues," accessed September 7, 2020, https://www. studyblue.com/notes/note/n/virtues/deck/19923071.
28. Webster's Dictionary 1828, s.v. "forgiveness," accessed September 7, 2020, http://webstersdictionary1828.com/ Dictionary/forgiveness.
29. Webster's Dictionary 1828, s.v. "diligence," accessed September 7, 2020, http://webstersdictionary1828.com/Dictionary/ diligence.
30. George Herbert, "Discipline," Poetry Foundation, accessed September 7, 2020, https://www.poetryfoundation.org/ poems/50702/discipline.
31. Webster's Dictionary 1828, s.v. "gentleness," accessed September 7, 2020, http://webstersdictionary1828.com/ Dictionary/gentleness.
32. Webster's Dictionary 1828, s.v. "equity," accessed September 8, 2020, http://webstersdictionary1828.com/Dictionary/equity.
33. Webster's Dictionary 1828, s.v. "truth," accessed September 8, 2020, http://webstersdictionary1828.com/Dictionary/truth.
34. Webster's Dictionary 1828, s.v. "mercy," accessed September 8, 2020, http://webstersdictionary1828.com/Dictionary/mercy.
35. Webster's Dictionary 1828, s.v. "mercy."
36. Webster's Dictionary 1828, s.v. "peaceableness," accessed September 8, 2020, http://webstersdictionary1828.com/ Dictionary/peaceableness.

37. Webster's Dictionary 1828, s.v. "godliness," accessed September 8, 2020, http://webstersdictionary1828.com/Dictionary/godliness.

38. Webster's Dictionary 1828, s.v. "cleanliness," accessed September 8, 2020, http://webstersdictionary1828.com/Dictionary/cleanliness.

39. Webster's Dictionary 1828, s.v. "orderliness," accessed September 8, 2020, http://webstersdictionary1828.com/Dictionary/Orderliness.

40. Wikipedia, s.v. "loyalty," accessed September 8, 2020, https://en.wikipedia.org/wiki/Loyalty.

41. Collins English Dictionary, s.v. "loyalty," accessed September 8, 2020, https://www.collinsdictionary.com/us/dictionary/english/loyalty.

42. Webster's Dictionary 1828, s.v. "faithfulness," accessed September 7, 2020, http://webstersdictionary1828.com/Dictionary/faithfulness.

43. Webster's Dictionary 1828, s.v. "faithfulness."

44. Webster's Dictionary 1828, s.v. "faithfulness."

45. "The Core Virtues of Faithfulness, Gentleness, and Self-Control," Agape Life Church Core Life Series, September 13, 2015, https://www.agapelife.org/hp_wordpress/wp-content/uploads/2015/09/2015-09-13.pdf.

46. Webster's Dictionary 1828, s.v. "charity," accessed September 7, 2020, http://webstersdictionary1828.com/Dictionary/charity.

47. Webster's Dictionary 1828, s.v. "charity."

48. Webster's Dictionary 1828, s.v. "charity."

49. Webster's Dictionary 1828, s.v. "charity."

50. Webster's Dictionary 1828, s.v. "reverence," accessed September 8, 2020, http://webstersdictionary1828.com/Dictionary/reverence.

51. Webster's Dictionary 1828, s.v. "reverence."

52. Webster's Dictionary 1828, s.v. "honesty," accessed September 8, 2020, http://webstersdictionary1828.com/Dictionary/honesty.

53. C. S. Lewis, *Mere Christianity* (New York: HarperOne, 2015), 95.

54. Webster's Dictionary 1828, s.v. "chastity," accessed September 7, 2020, http://webstersdictionary1828.com/Dictionary/chastity.

55. Webster's Dictionary 1828, s.v. "chastity."

56. Webster's Dictionary 1828, s.v. "chastity."

57. Webster's Dictionary 1828, s.v. "chastity."

58. Webster's Dictionary 1828, s.v. "hope," accessed September 7, 2020, http://webstersdictionary1828.com/Dictionary/hope.

59. Webster's Dictionary 1828, s.v. "hope."

60. Webster's Dictionary 1828, s.v. "hope."

61. Webster's Dictionary 1828, s.v. "faith," accessed September 8, 2020, http://webstersdictionary1828.com/Dictionary/faith.

62. This quote is often attributed to Charles Caleb Colton. (See, for instance, ForbesQuotes, "Thoughts on the Business of Life," accessed September 8, 2020, https://www.forbes.com/quotes/1905/.) But it is also quoted by Thomas Joseph Sullivan in *Merchants and Manufacturers on Trial* (Chicago: Thomas J. Sullivan Company, 1914), 59.

63. Webster's Dictionary 1828, s.v. "integrity," accessed September 8, 2020, http://webstersdictionary1828.com/Dictionary/integrity.

64. Kerby Anderson, "Integrity—A Christian Virtue," Probe Ministries International, May 27, 2000, https://probe.org/integrity/.

65. Webster's Dictionary 1828, s.v. "gratitude," accessed September 8, 2020, http://webstersdictionary1828.com/Dictionary/gratitude.

66. Webster's Dictionary 1828, s.v. "sincerity," accessed September 8, 2020, http://webstersdictionary1828.com/Dictionary/sincerity.

67. Michael Hickey, *Get Goodness: Virtue Is the Power to Do Good* (Lanham, MD: University Press of America, 2011).

68. Webster's Dictionary 1828, s.v. "goodness," accessed September 8, 2020, http://webstersdictionary1828.com/Dictionary/goodness.
69. Webster's Dictionary 1828, s.v. "goodness."
70. Webster's Dictionary 1828, s.v. "hospitality," accessed September 8, 2020, http://webstersdictionary1828.com/Dictionary/hospitality.
71. *Merriam-Webster*, s.v. "hospitable," accessed September 8, 2020, https://www.merriam-webster.com/dictionary/hospitable.

CHAPTER 7

1. *Merriam-Webster*, s.v. "long-suffering," accessed September 8, 2020, https://www.merriam-webster.com/dictionary/long-suffering.
2. "Christian Persecution at 'Near Genocide Levels,'" BBC News, May 3, 2019, https://www.bbc.com/news/uk-48146305.
3. Bill Vincent, *Glory: Expanding God's Presence* (Litchfield, IL: Revival Waves of Glory, 2016), 98.

CHAPTER 8

1. Blue Letter Bible, s.v. *"techor,"* accessed September 7, 2020, https://www.blueletterbible.org/lang/lexicon/lexicon.cfm?Strongs=H2914&t=KJV.